Gold, Frankincense, and Myrrh

Gold, Frankincense, and Myrrh

AN INTRODUCTION TO EASTERN CHRISTIAN SPIRITUALITY

GEORGE A. MALONEY

A Crossroad Book
The Crossroad Publishing Company
New York

Imprimi Potest:
Rev. Bert R. Thelen, S.J.
Provincial Superior, Wisconsin Province

1997

The Crossroad Publishing Company
370 Lexington Avenue, New York, NY 10017

Library of Congress Cataloging-in-Publication Data
Maloney, George A., 1924-
    Gold, frankincense, and myrrh : an introduction to Eastern
Christian spirituality / George A. Maloney.
      p. cm.
    Includes bibliographical references and index.
    ISBN 0-8245-1616-8 (pbk.)
    1. Spirituality – Orthodox Eastern Church. 2. Orthodox Eastern
Church – Doctrines. I. Title.
BX382.M35 1997
248'.088'219–dc21   97-4141
                                                CIP

To Mary Flaherty,
mother of fifteen children, of many grandchildren,
and spiritual mother to innumerable neophyte Christians
through her RCIA apostolate in her parish

Contents

Acknowledgments

Sincerest thanks to Cyndy and Bill Murphy for teaching me the "mysteries" of the Mac computer; to June Culver for her encouragement and help in proofreading this text.

Grateful acknowledgment to the Byzantine Seminary Press for permission to use the drawings in the text. They are from the Byzantine Coloring Books *Sunday Gospels* (© 1990) and *Feast Days* (© 1977) sketched by Father John Matusiak. These books are available from Byzantine Seminary Press, 3605 Perrysville Avenue, P.O. Box 7626, Pittsburgh, PA 15214.

Grateful acknowledgment is made to the publishers, Darton, Longman & Todd, Ltd., and Doubleday & Company, Inc., New York, for excerpts from the Jerusalem Bible, copyright 1966.

Preface

W HAT DO YOU SUPPOSE would happen to the Church of Jesus Christ if a group of well-educated men and women, skilled in philosophy, literature, the arts, and science, were to go out into the stark, wild deserts of the world and there spend their days and nights for years falling down before the Burning Bush of God's never-consuming love and adoring him with all their heart? Imagine what type of Christianity might prevail throughout our modern world if, after years of purifying themselves to experience God's uncreated energies, these "Christians intoxicated with God's love" (to use the term Pseudo-Macarius applied to the desert hermits of the fourth century) were to return to society and become enlightened teachers?

From the fourth to the eighth centuries, the above scenario became a reality with the desert Fathers and Mothers of the Church. Most of these inspired teachers first had to become purified vessels of the Holy Spirit, who taught them *true theology*. They fought valiantly against heresies aimed at destroying the true revelation of God unveiled by the Word made flesh, Jesus Christ, in and through his Holy Spirit. These great ascetics and mystics gave us the Nicene-Constantinopolitan Creed and the definitive statements of the first seven ecumenical councils from the fourth through the eighth centuries.

Many of these teachers were greatly persecuted for the truths to which we now often render mere intellectual assent, such as the true divinity of Christ, who is "of the same substance as the Father," as defined in the Councils of Nicaea (325) and Constantinople (381). In the following five ecumenical councils the divinity of the Holy Spirit, as well as the hypostatic union of Christ, was defined: one person in two natures, distinct but not separable and not absorbed one into the other.

In the seventh ecumenical council in 787 the sacredness of icons was recognized by the Fathers as a point of reverence and devotion to the Trinity, Jesus Christ, Mary the Theotokos, or "Birthgiver to God," the angels and the saints.

These successors of the first apostles of Christ knew that *orthodoxia,* or "right teaching," handed down to them had to be free of error since it came from God, who is Truth. Therefore, they called their way *orthopraxis* or "right living." They became "Fathers" for all generations of Christians since they were chosen instruments of God to aid us in becoming children of the one true "Father over us all" (Eph. 4:6).

The orthodoxy of the teachings of these early Fathers was one with the teachings of Christ's first apostles. They manifested a holiness in their lives as both mystics and theologians because they really experienced what they taught. They lived out what Evagrius of the fourth-century Egyptian desert wrote: "If you pray, you will be a *theologian*. If you are a *theologian*, you will pray." They also gained the universal approval of the Church as true teachers who witnessed in their writings to the authentic traditions stemming from the early disciples of Christ.

Finally, they possessed the quality of antiquity, having lived in the first eight centuries of Christianity and fought for the formation of the apostolic traditions, especially through the teachings affirmed by many of them who participated directly or through their writings in the first seven ecumenical councils, all held in the Greek-speaking world of the Christian East.

The Eastern Churches

When we use the term "Eastern Christian Churches," we refer to those Christian Churches which evolved in the eastern half of the then Roman Empire in the first five centuries of Christianity and others that were dependent upon those beginning Churches, even though the daughter Churches were and still are now found outside of the original boundaries of the Roman Empire. The chief centers of civil administration became the ecclesiastical centers since Christianity flourished mostly in populated urban centers.

All Eastern Churches evolved from the Patriarchates of Constantinople, Alexandria, and Antioch, and the two Churches of Persia and Armenia, which developed outside the Roman Empire. Thus we find the roots of the five leading Eastern Christian Churches correspond to five ecclesiastical jurisdictions, namely, the Byzantine, Alexandrian, Antiochene (or Western Syrian), East Syrian, and Armenian.

The East Syrian, or Assyrian, Church was formed through the fifth-century heresy called *Nestorianism*, which was condemned at the Ecumenical Council of Ephesus in 431. At the Council of Chalcedon in 451 the heresy of *Monophysitism*, which taught that the human nature of Jesus was absorbed into his divinity, was condemned. This resulted in the formation of the Armenian, Coptic, and Syrian Churches, often referred to as *Orientals*.

These Churches no longer belonged to the "one, holy, catholic, and apostolic Church" as did the remaining Eastern Orthodox Byzantine and Roman Churches. Through a gradual estrangement, climaxed by the Latin Crusaders who sacked Constantinople in 1204 and the disputes about the primacy in jurisdiction of the Pope of Rome over the other Eastern Patriarchs, there resulted the *schism* that divided the Roman and the Byzantine Orthodox Churches from each other.

A great missionary effort, led by Jesuits, Dominicans, and Franciscans, working in those Eastern countries from the sixteenth century into modern times, strove to "reunite" certain Eastern Churches with Rome. Rome promised such Orthodox and Oriental Church leaders that their liturgical rituals and elements of their canonical disciplines could be preserved. This policy has been given the term "uniatism."

Map of the Journey

For many years I have longed to write this type of a book. I have been personally enriched from my years of studying the Eastern Christian Fathers, teaching their writings in colleges and universities for some twenty-five years and writing some fifty-five books, all inspired by the rich mystical insights of the Eastern Fathers. Yet this has been a most difficult book for me to write.

How does one go about synthesizing the mountains of writings of these literary giants? Could an author ever do justice to interpreting such treasures of traditions from the early centuries of Christianity for modern Christians? I have struggled to choose the themes which I thought were representative of the unique riches of Eastern Christian spirituality. There was an inevitable frustration in not being able to include other equally important patristic topics, so essential to the common Eastern patristic treasury. On the other hand, choices had to be made in order to keep this book from becoming another "series" of patristic texts rather than simply a humble offering of what I personally feel are areas of the Christian life that would be most beneficial to Roman Catholics, Orthodox, and Protestants living in Western countries, to whom the writings of the Eastern Fathers are practically unknown.

There are two ways of describing the path of spiritual perfection according to the traditions found in Eastern Christianity. One method, as used by Dr. John Chirban,[1] is to study the writings of individual Eastern theologians and mystics who lived experientially such a spiritual process of growing in union with God and then work out the elements that seemingly fit into the various stages.

This seems to be an attempt to violate the dynamic features of the writers of Eastern Christian spirituality, who realized that the Holy Spirit works in many various ways, not to be classified in static stages that would necessarily have to be universal and applicable to the progress of each serious Christian, a method we have often seen in description of the spiritual life in Western Christianity.

I have chosen a more fluid approach (and one that I believe is more closely in line with the "apophatic" spirit found in the writings of the Eastern Fathers), which opposes any logical description or scheme to describe the various stages of perfection in the spiritual life. Thus I have drawn from the large corpus of Eastern Christian writers those elements that commonly make up the traditional orthodoxy of the Christian East.

There is a progress presented in my proposed journey, but I believe it adheres more to the traditional approach of the giants of Eastern Christianity, both the mystics and the mystical theologians. Thus the first five chapters reflect on God-Trinity's intimate relationship with us human beings and God's created world. I start this journey by focusing on the "fourth dimension" vision from within the very heart of God as trinitarian. Chapter 1 leads us into the exuberant love of the Trinity that freely explodes outward to create a world immersed in the ocean of the Trinity's personalized love for us.

Chapter 2 develops one of the most basic scriptural themes out of which the Eastern Fathers universally evolved a theological anthropology, namely, that we are made "according to the image and likeness" of God in and through Jesus Christ and the Holy Spirit.

To avoid any dry speculation about God in relation to us human beings, we then study in chapter 3 what I consider a most important Eastern corrective to Western theology, namely, the "apophatic" way. Admitting the important but limited value of positive speculative theology, the Eastern Fathers, mystics that they were, insisted on an *apophatic* theology as a positive knowledge given by the Holy Spirit to the "poor in spirit." This is a knowledge beyond all human understanding attained through the "cloud of unknowing."

By studying the Logos mysticism of these early Eastern Fathers chapter 4 links the mystery of the incarnation and the contemplation of Christ, the Logos enfleshed. Chapter 5 deals with one of the most important contributions of the Eastern Fathers to present-day Christian spirituality, i.e., the understanding that God-Trinity communicates with us human beings through the uncreated energies of divine love.

Chapters 6, 7, and 8 develop the Fathers' teachings on sin and its effects upon us and the universe, as well as the need to enter into a continued process of conversion through weeping and contrition for our sins and our own cooperation through *praxis,* or the ascetical life.

Chapter 9 presents the cosmic dimension of Christ through his resurrectional presence in the Church and the patristic teaching on Christ's role as Recapitulator of all creation into its fullness in him.

In chapter 10 we look at Mary as the microcosmic archetype of the Church and of each individual Christian living in Christ. In chapter 11 we apply the orthodox teaching about Jesus Christ as one divine person in two distinct natures, both divine and human, by studying the theology and the experienced encounters with the risen Christ and the divinized world of the angels and saints through the Eastern veneration of *icons*. The final chapter highlights the personal role of the hidden, kenotic Holy Spirit as the gift of love from the Father and Son that will make us holy cocreators with Christ of a "new creation."

Breathing with Two Lungs

Pope John Paul II has often quoted the statement of the Dominican theologian Yves Congar that Christians today must breathe with two lungs: the spirituality of the Christian West and that of the East. Would you not agree with me that most of us Christians in the West have little knowledge of the more ancient and most valid traditions that link us back to the first "one, holy, and *apostolic* Church" of the early apostles of Christ?

I would hope and pray that this book will prove to be very helpful for Christians eagerly seeking to grow more deeply in the Christian spiritual life. May it open you up to breathe with two lungs and discover what it means to become, in the words of the second-century theologian St. Irenaeus, fully alive spiritually: "The glory of God is a human being living fully." *Breathing fully!*

CHAPTER ONE

The Holy Trinity: Mysticism of Community

IN INGMAR BERGMAN'S MOVIE *Winter Light,* Pastor Tomas Eriksson seeks to give consolation, encouragement, and counsel to one of his parishioners, a fear-tormented fisherman by the name of Jonas Persson. Persson is in anguish over his conviction that the Chinese are about to obtain the atom bomb with which they will bring about the eventual nuclear destruction of the world. The Lutheran pastor, with all his clichés and high-sounding phrases, is unable to touch the fisherman's heart and bring him peace. "If I speak with human tongues and angelic as well, but do not have love, I am a noisy gong, a clanging cymbal" (1 Cor. 13:1).

The main point of Bergman's movie is that if we are to be re-deemed, it must be by the strong, persistent love of God, who cloaks himself in deep silence before our selfish, bombastic questionings about God and ourselves and our world. We have been made by God for communion, a "union with" God and all human beings. Another way of putting it is to describe God as a loving community of persons who wish to share their trinitarian life as we experience their divine love in each event of each day. We begin to move toward loving communion with God and neighbor by means of "communication." The first step of communication is to relay information to another on a linear level. Such knowledge tends to deal with logical facts, ideas that are comprehensible to our human reasoning. Our sciences are examples of such communication. Making theology exclusively a "science" is another example of such knowledge.

Language of the Heart

But there is a higher level of knowledge. This is *communion* between friends and lovers, between ourselves and our loving God. It is the language of the human heart in which love mysteriously speaks and makes the loved one present as a gift to the other. There can be no array of logical proof that will ever bring about such a communion. It is a surrendering love built upon faith and hope in the one loved.

We can say that we human beings have been made by God to become "present" to the trinitarian communitarian love and to each other by the love of God that is constantly being poured out into our hearts by the Holy Spirit, as St. Paul writes in Romans 5:5. We were made for love, for communion with God and the whole world in the unity of God's Word. This is the great craving placed into our hearts by God. This, we could say, is the presence of God as uncreated energies of love, moving us by his

Spirit toward greater and greater union with God and all of God's creation.

On the eve of the third millennium, we stand before God and shout out with rage our demands that he speak to us as we would wish him to speak. But all we hear in reply is the echo of our own self-centered musings. We have effectively lost the ability to recognize the voice of God as he speaks his Word to us in silence and in love. We hear instead the insidious promptings of the demonic within us that, like a boa constrictor, wraps itself around our throats and suffocates us in a kind of living death. Such is the only silence most of us ever experience. It is the silence created by the absence of speech and the lack of true communication in love between us and God and all other human persons.

Søren Kierkegaard, the great Danish philosopher, wrote about such genuine silence and the urgency on our part to attain it when he stated:

> The present state of the world and the whole of life is diseased. If I were a doctor and were asked for my advice, I should reply: Create Silence! Bring men to silence. The Word of God cannot be heard in the noisy world of today. And even if it were blazoned forth with all the panoply of noise so that it could be heard in the midst of all the other noise, then it would no longer be the Word of God. Therefore, create silence.[1]

In loving another, we become a gifted presence to that person. We wish to live in union, the true meaning of *communion*, with that person so as to be present as often and as intimate as possible, not only physically in space and time, but more importantly in the inner recesses of our consciousness. We are this way because God is this way in his essence as love (1 John 4:8).

The Trinitarian Community

God the Father, in absolute silence, in a communication of love impossible for us human beings to understand, speaks his one eternal Word through his Spirit of love. In that one Word, the Father is perfectly present, totally self-giving to his Son. "In him lives the fullness of divinity" (Col. 2:9). But in his Spirit, the Father also hears his Word come back to him in a perfect, eternal "yes" of total surrendering love that is again the Holy Spirit.

The Trinity is a reciprocal community of a movement of the Spirit of love between Father and Son. Our weak minds cannot fathom the peace and joy, the ardent excitement and exuberant self-surrender that flow in a reposeful motion between Father and Son through the silent Holy Spirit. God becomes real only because he can communicate in love through his Word. His Word gives him his identity as Father. But that means eternal self-giving to the Other, his Word in love, the Holy Spirit.

Whatever human words may be used to penetrate somewhat the inner mystery of God's nature as love in a communion of persons, our attitude demands something of the *apophatic* approach as we shall see in a more detailed treatment in chapter 3. This is more than a negation of whatever we can positively assert through rational knowledge about the attributes of God. But the apophatic knowledge is knowledge given to us by the Holy Spirit that goes beyond all human knowledge (Eph. 3:17–18).

The Eastern Fathers learned well from Holy Scripture and from their own sense of brokenness in prayer that only God can lead us into the mystery of God's nature as love. We must realize that we cannot comprehend God's inner life completely or we would have to be part of the family of God by our very nature. Yet Scripture insists that we can know this Trinity by "not knowing." In our poverty and utter creatureliness, in our sinfulness and alienation from the heavenly Father, we realize that to know God is beyond our power. "No one has ever seen God; it is the only Son, who is nearest to the Father's heart, who has made him known" (John 1:18).

Yet the Good News revealed by the Word made flesh, Jesus Christ, is that we can come to know the Father through the Son: "And eternal life is this: to know you, the only true God, and Jesus Christ whom you have sent" (John 17:3). As we Christians grow in contemplation, we realize more and more that God must reveal himself to us. We can only wait in the desert of our nothingness, hoping to receive God as he wishes to make himself known to us. With the humility of children, we seek entrance into the heart of God as he communicates himself to his Word through his Spirit of love. This is the teaching of Jesus who speaks about the possibility of such children receiving, not merely knowledge or a communication, but the privilege in contemplation to enter into the very trinitarian "communion." "I bless you, Father, Lord of heaven and of earth, for hiding these things from the learned and the clever and revealing them to mere children" (Matt. 11:25).

God's Word incarnate, Jesus Christ, by his death and resurrection is now a living Word dwelling within us along with his Holy Spirit. He not only gives us the elements that constitute God's inner life, but he makes it possible through his Spirit that those elements can also be experienced by us.

Thus this trinitarian reality is to be experienced *now.* The doctrine of the Trinity is not only what makes Christianity uniquely different from all other religions, but it is a reality that effects the fulfillment of our very being as human persons. Christology and all other dogmas, Liturgy and the sacraments, preaching the Gospel and developing the Christian life of Christlike virtues all have their meaning and subordination to this central teaching of the Trinity. We are baptized in the Father, Son, and Spirit. We profess in faith that, even as infants, we were receiving God's trinitarian actions upon us. We are confirmed, reconciled to God, ordained, married, healed in the name of the three divine persons. We bless ourselves in the Trinity and seek to do all for the glory of the Trinity. God revealed this mystery to us in order that he might humbly share the secret of his own intimate life with us. This reality is meant to be a living experience for us. We are to live in this teaching. But unfortunately for too many centuries the precisions of professional theologians dominated our approach to the Trinity. We were rooted more in Aristotelian philosophy than in Holy Scripture. It is God's living Word who alone can reveal to us this awesome reality and make it effective and transformative in our lives.

Karl Rahner laments that most Christians believe in a "monotheistic God" while they give a merely intellectual assent to the doctrine of the Trinity without truly experiencing the three divine persons in their one nature of love:

> Despite their orthodox confession of the Trinity, Christians are, in their practical life, almost mere "monotheists." We must be willing to admit that, should the doctrine of the Trinity have to be dropped as false, the major part of religious literature could well remain virtually unchanged.[2]

The Richness of the Godhead

In God we see that silence is not opposed to words, but true Word-communication comes from the silence of the Spirit of love and continues to be spoken and lived out in the same silence of the Spirit. Perhaps a good way to understand God's communicative silence is to study the classic Byzantine icon of the Trinity painted by the Russian monk Andrei Rublev (c. 1408–25).

This painting is a mystical vision, through harmony and relationship of colors and circular lines, of the inner trinitarian life of movement and rest, peace and joy, a community of three in one. The Godhead is a nameless form which constantly feeds back through its circular movement from one person to the other two. In this icon we see three angels, the heavenly visitors to Abraham at the oak of Mambre (Gen. 18), depicting the three persons of the Trinity. The Father is shown as the angel on the left, as a figure subdued and retiring, suggesting the apophatic belief in the direct unknowability of the Father or the Godhead of the Trinity, except through the Son, who is the angelic figure in the center. He dominates the entire icon as he gazes lovingly at the Father while pointing his two fingers, symbolic of his two natures, divine and human, toward the eucharistic chalice on the white table before them.

The Holy Spirit is seen as the third angel, on the right, dressed in a green cloak, the sign of youth and fullness of powers. Before there are divine persons, in intercommunion with each other in expressed love, there is the Godhead. The Eastern Fathers begin with the Godhead, as the "unoriginated Source," the principal root of unity in the Trinity. St. Gregory of Nazianzus, the great fourth-century Greek theologian who wrote so eloquently about the Trinity, describes the Father as the source and goal of diversity or personal relationships within the Trinity:

> The nature is one in three; it is God; but that which makes the unity is the Father, from whom and to whom the order of persons runs its course, not in such a way that the nature is confused, but that it is possessed without distinction of time or of will or of power.[3]

This Godhead is the Abyss of silence. It is not nonbeing out of which comes the being of the three persons. It is God as "unnatured nature," to use Meister Eckhart's phrase. It is nonbeing for it contains all beings. It is *nowhere* for it cannot be contained in its wildness before it becomes tamed by love. It is the ocean before fish have been created. It is the air before birds have been made to fly. It is the fullness of the *Uncreated* before the spark ignites and hurls intelligence toward loving union. It is where total poverty meets infinite richness. It is *Infinite Zero* from which everyone and everything radiates and to which all lovingly return.

Because of the Godhead's infinite richness, it cannot be classified in quantified numbers or in categories of beings that have an origin of their being. The Godhead is beyond all being and yet is found in all being, including the Trinity and ourselves. Nietzsche once wrote: "One must possess a chaos within to give birth to a star."[4] It is here that the Father becomes the Father of his Son through the silent love of the Holy Spirit, who proceeds from both the Father and the Son. Two looks devoured by love! It is here that we are led in silent adoration and contemplation to a knowing beyond our knowing.

In silence we come into the *Void*. We merge with the darkness of the Godhead. No longer is God an "object" toward which we go in prayer to communicate in order to receive some "things." The ocean covers everything and does not need to become wet since all things are wet because of its complete covering of everything.

Like the crackling sound of a fiery spark that shoots through the rain-soaked heavens, a movement stirs within nonmovement. A light moves through darkness. Out of the Void God stirs as personal Source, the Father, who wishes from all eternity to share his fullness of being. The Mind wishes to think a thought, to speak a word, in order to know himself as the Begetter of the Word.

The Father moves the Godhead from pure repose and absolute silence to meaningful, loving motion, as he pours the fullness of his divinity into his Son (Col. 2:9). What we could never know, God's Word has revealed to us. God is a loving community, a family of loving persons, each person receiving his uniqueness by self-emptying gift of total self to the other in and through the gift of love itself, the Spirit.

It is an ecstatic, loving intimacy of the Father emptying himself into his Son through his Spirit of love. Such intimacy and self-emptying are returned by the Son's gifting himself back to the Father through the same Spirit. Jesus reveals that in the Trinity is the secret of life which unfolds in silence, the language of love. Love is a call to receive one's *being* in the intimate self-surrendering of the other. In the ecstasy of "standing outside" of oneself and becoming available through the gift of love to live for the other, Father and Son and Holy Spirit, all come into their unique personhood as distinct yet united persons.[5]

The *I* is the child of the *We,* as Gabriel Marcel applies the mystery of true love in the Trinity and in our human love relationships.[6] God as Trinity is the revelation that uniqueness of persons comes only from a family of two or more persons in love. In the very self-giving of the Father to the Son and the Son to the Father a third Person has his unique *personhood,* the Holy Spirit. He proceeds, not as another Word, but from the silent love of the Father for the Son and the single, silent Word, the Son, surrendering to the Father. The Spirit is silent love, experienced, but not heard except in the soundlessness of love itself.

Silence in the Trinity

The awesome mystery of the Trinity, which is the beginning and the end of all reality, reveals to us a transcendent truth that should permeate our entire lives. Out of Absolute Silence the Godhead could not yet experience community. For an *I-Thou* relationship, bringing forth a *We*-community, could come only when the Father spoke in relative silence his Word. That *relative* silence we call the Holy Spirit, the binding, self-sacrificing love between the Father and the Son.

The Spirit is the cosmic bird that hovers over the chaos and the void. It stirs the *I* of the heavenly Father to perceive himself as one not isolated. The Spirit who is the Spirit of love, moves the heart of the Father, and the Son is begotten in the silent Word that the Father utters. The Father thrills to see himself imaged, as Mind discovers itself in the Word that issues from the Mind. But he thrills also to discover himself as the unique Father of his Son when the Son in the power of the silent Spirit utters his silent *Yes* in total self-surrender to the Father.

We — patterned on God's image and likeness (Gen. 1:26) —

project that image most often, not in the negative silence of
chosen isolation and mutism, but in speech. But the words we
speak must proceed from the same silent Spirit of love and return
"home" to that Spirit. We move away from imaging God as he
speaks his Word in the silent love of the Spirit when we fail to
speak our words in God's love.

It is through God's Spirit of love that he has the name of "Father." His fatherhood is expressed in his silent, eternal self-giving
to his Son. St. Hilary of Poitiers insists that the Father and the
Son have a perfect mutual relationship of Father and Son to each
other.[7] If the Father and Son mutually know themselves, this is
brought about necessarily by the Holy Spirit, who allows them
in silence, not only to affirm themselves as Father and Son, but
mutually to recognize themselves as such.

From this threefold movement, therefore, all reality within the
Trinity and outside in all of creation flows through the Trinity's
uncreated energies of love (see chapter 5). Such an "implosion" of
love between Father and Son through the Spirit within the Trinity
seemingly is not enough. Such tremendous love within the Trinity,
we learn only from Scripture, seeks to "explode" outside of its
own community. God freely wishes to create new life that can
share in the divine, ecstatic love within the Trinity.

We human beings know this to be our experience of an authentic *I-Thou* love relationship that stretches outward to share that
love in new human love with another in the creation of new life.
This is true because it is first true of God, the Source of all participated life and love. When we love one another, God's love in us
is being perfected (1 John 4:12).

It is only faith received through God's revelation found in the
Old and New Testaments that opens us to accept the Good News
that the trinitarian community of Father, Son, and Holy Spirit
moves outward freely to create a world of participated beauty.
Yet of all God's material creatures we human beings are gifted to
be able to communicate with the Trinity by sharing in God's very
own nature (2 Pet. 1:4). We are called in God's gratuitous love

to receive the divine, self-emptying love as self-gift of Father and Son and Holy Spirit.

Our calling is to enter into God's primal silence and hear his Word of love, Jesus Christ, tell us at each moment of our earthly journey how great is his love. We are called to answer in the shared silence of the Word as we, with him, repeat our constant "Yes!" in total silence.

The Divine Economy

We see, therefore, that the ineffable mystery of the Trinity, that which escapes our own human comprehension, can, however, be known and experienced in and through Jesus Christ and the Holy Spirit. God not only deemed to reveal the truth of this mystery to us, but in that revelation he has made the mystery of the Trinity the beginning and end of all reality. God effects our fulfillment precisely in and through the activities of the triune God in the context of our history of salvation.

We come, not only to know, but also to experience the triune God within what Karl Rahner calls the biblical data about the "economic" Trinity. "Economia" (*oikonomia* in Greek) etymologically refers to running a household well.[8] In theology it usually refers to any divine activity in relationship to creatures. Thus theologians speak of "the economy of salvation." Among the Eastern Fathers *theology* properly so-called concerns itself with teaching about the divine Being itself, namely, the Holy Trinity known in its relation to created beings. This belongs vitally to the realm of the economy of salvation.[9]

Karl Rahner states very emphatically his principle that he maintains is the persistent teaching of the Eastern Fathers of the relationship of the Trinity toward us human beings made in God's image in the history of salvation. "The 'economic Trinity' is the 'immanent Trinity' and the 'immanent Trinity' is the 'economic Trinity.' "[10] This means that the very relationships within the Trinity (immanent Trinity) are the same relationships of the Trinity in bringing about God's eternal plan of salvation.

In identifying the Trinity of the economy of salvation with the very life within the Trinity of Father, Son, and Holy Spirit, Rahner seeks to recapture the fundamental teaching of the Eastern Fathers that the personalism of the three divine persons toward each other in their self-giving is similar to their self-giving relationships to us human beings. If this were not so, Rahner argues: "God would be the 'giver,' not the gift itself. He would 'give himself' only to the extent that he communicates a gift distinct from himself."[11]

Upon this Eastern Christian teaching of the similarity between the immanent, trinitarian "activities" and the "economic activities" hinges the answer to the question: Are we human beings so loved by God that we are able to be radically transformed by God's very gift of himself by the Trinity's very own transforming persons of Father, Son, and Spirit? If God merely loves us to the degree that he gives us created gifts, we would never be truly saved from our sins and be regenerated into true children of God.

Crucial in this patristic doctrine is that through God's uncreated energies of love we actually do make contact with the living Trinity. God is truly love. The community of the Trinity wants to share its perfect love of self-giving within the Trinity with us human beings by transforming us into sharers of God's very own nature (2 Pet. 1:4) St. Irenaeus of the second century pictures God as coming toward us in the created world through his two hands: Jesus Christ and the Holy Spirit: "And therefore throughout all time, man, having been molded at the beginning by the hands of God, that is, of the Son and the Spirit, is made after the image and likeness of God."[12]

God is grace! He gives us this sharing in the Trinity's life through the uncreated energies that are the personalized, self-giving of the Father and Son and Holy Spirit to us. It is this moving of God's We-community toward us that gives us a share in the very life of the three persons that is at the heart of the

Christian message and the chief purpose of Christ's incarnation, teaching, and death on the cross, and the outpouring of the Holy Spirit.

It is for this reason that the Eastern Christian theologians, mystics that they were, always began with the first words of the book of Genesis: "In the beginning, God...." It is for this reason that we should be grounded firmly in the great mystery of the Holy Trinity since all other chapters in this book and all our other relationships flow out of this mystery of the Trinity. In prayerful humility and a sense of our deep unworthiness to approach God in order to probe into *how* God communicates himself to us, we can turn to that intimate, trinitarian union of love to which God calls us.

It is a path that leads us beyond idols and images, even beyond our objectivizing God as a Person to whom we can address ourselves as to another created being. It is a knowledge of experience that admits of an infinite growth because this knowledge surpasses all human understanding and becomes identified with true love. To know the Trinity in this sense of mystery is to love God through the Spirit of Jesus Christ as God loves us.

St. Paul's statement in his letter to the Ephesians can serve to summarize in nonspeculative, scriptural terms the movement of the divine We-community into our world in order to share with us human beings the same relationships enjoyed between Father and Son as I-Thou, brought together in perfect, loving union by the Spirit:

Blessed be God the Father of our Lord Jesus Christ,
who has blessed us with all the spiritual blessings of heaven
   in Christ.
Before the world was made, he chose us, chose us in Christ,
to be holy and spotless, and to live through love in his
   presence,
determining that we should become his adopted sons,
   through Jesus Christ...

to make us praise the glory of his grace,
his free gift to us in the Beloved....
He has let us know the mystery of his purpose,
the hidden plan he so kindly made in Christ
from the beginning....
Now you too, in him,
have heard the message of the truth and the good news of
    your salvation,
and have believed it;
and you too have been stamped with the seal of the Holy
    Spirit of the Promise,
the pledge of our inheritance
which brings freedom for those whom God has taken for his
    own,
to make his glory praised. (Eph. 1:3–14)

CHAPTER TWO

Made in God's Image and Likeness

I N THAT DELIGHTFUL modern parable entitled *Jonathan Livingston Seagull,* an instructing seagull explains to Jonathan Livingston, the young seagull: "You've got to understand that a seagull is an unlimited idea of freedom, an image of the Great Gull, and your whole body, from wingtip to wingtip, is nothing more than your thought itself." In another passage the instructing seagull explains what is needed to reach fulfillment as a seagull: "The hardest thing in the world is to convince a bird that he is free and that he can prove it for himself if he'd just spend a little time practicing. Why should that be so hard?"[1]

33

You and I have been made by God-Trinity to be free, to share in the Trinity's freedom to love each other in complete self-giving to each other through the binding, self-emptying Holy Spirit. This makes us unique among all the other creatures, called by God to be the lord and master, the faithful steward as a willing being, ordered toward God's love, as prophet and priest. Through Jesus we are capable of communing with our Maker and cocreating with God-Trinity in transfiguring the created elements of this cosmos into signs of our loving surrender to our Maker and Father through the Son of God in their mutual Holy Spirit.

Our uniqueness over all creation consists in our God-given power to be self-positing. We have been ordained by God's creation to a living, dynamic relationship in self-surrendering love to the triune community of Father, Son, and Holy Spirit. We are made, as both male and female, according to God's own image and likeness (Gen. 1:26–27). God is continually in the process of creating us in such a way that we are being constantly summoned to receive God's Word actively. We are called to listen, to understand, and to believe in God's intimate communicating with us through his Word made flesh, Jesus Christ, in and through their Spirit. Our unique being as an "I" is being from and in the divine Word through whom all things are made (John 1:2).

We are obligated in our freedom to answer God's call. We are beings created by God, in the words of Emil Brunner, "to stand 'over against' God, and reply to God. In our answer alone we can fulfill or destroy God's purpose in creating us."[2]

A Return to the Early Fathers of the Church

There is a strong renaissance of Christian mysticism developing throughout our modern world. This will also bring about a return to the basic insights of the early Fathers, especially of the Christian East, whose theology was primarily the fruit of their deep, mystical prayer-life. Holy Scripture, especially the writings of St. John and St. Paul, became for them the living Word of God and gave them a solid theological anthropology of human persons as seen from God's creative viewpoint.

Such charismatic giants, purified by years of monastic asceticism, spoke from their Spirit-filled experiences of divinization, which they called *theosis*. They had experienced in prayer a dynamic process of growth from a potential relationship to God through Jesus Christ to an ever-increasing consciousness through the infusion of the Holy Spirit's gifts of faith, hope, and love of being assimilated into the ocean of the Trinity's allness.

The early Eastern patristic writers developed their whole doctrine of grace, of creation, their theological anthropology and human psychology, and therefore their whole understanding of the ascetical and mystical life around the image and likeness doctrine. Among Catholic, Protestant, and Orthodox scholars there is taking place a rebirth of patristic studies because of the innate conviction that these early Eastern Fathers grasped as in no other age the understanding of pristine Christianity, especially as expounded in the writings of St. John and St. Paul.

The earliest Christians were mainly concerned with living the new-found faith in simple obedience to the message of the Gospel. Gradually, as they explained their faith to neighboring pagans and Jews or defended Christ's revelation from heretical teachings, there developed an articulated tradition that would be made up of reflective knowledge concerning the basic truths of the Christian faith.

The early Eastern Fathers built up a theology of divinization around two terms found in Gen. 1:26: "Let us make man according to our image and likeness" (*eikon*, image, and *homoiosis*, likeness). We find in their speculation about these two concepts the meeting of an integrated theology of Christ and the Trinity, God's creation and his goal in creating all things in his Word, sin and the dynamic expression of salvation and redemption through divine grace.

The Septuagint, or Greek Old Testament, does not say that we human beings *are* the "image and likeness" of God. We are made only *according to* the image and likeness of God. St. Paul tells us that only Jesus Christ is the icon, or image, of God:

> He is the image of the unseen God and the first-born of all creation, for in him were created all things in heaven and on earth: everything visible and invisible. All things were created through him and for him. Before anything was created he existed, and he holds all things in unity. (Col. 1:15–20)

Thus we see that Eastern Christian spirituality is deeply rooted in the central faith of the Holy Trinity. God, the source of all existence, the Father, Son, and Holy Spirit, created human beings according to the image and likeness that is Jesus Christ, both God and man. The process of moving into a more conscious, loving relationship to God the Father, which means an ontological life of Christ living within us, is effected through the sanctifying activity of the Holy Spirit.

St. Cyril of Alexandria shows, however, that these actions and operations of bringing us human beings into the fullness of God's divine life are effected by the whole Trinity: Father, Son, and Holy Spirit. "All things come from the Father through the Son in the Holy Spirit."[3] Nothing of divine operation in the created order is attributed solely to any individual person of the Trinity, but such action responds to the intertrinitarian relations.[4]

All Christians Are Called to Be Holy

The process of moving from image to likeness in divinization is the end, therefore, of every human being in God's eternal plan. The Fathers did not hold a distinction between precepts of obligation, binding all Christians, and evangelical counsels which are followed only by monks and those who embrace the religious life of the vows of poverty, chastity, and obedience.

St. Basil, St. John Chrysostom, and others insisted that all Christians are to be *monotropoi,* i.e., monks, from the word *monachos,* which fundamentally means an integrated, whole person according to God's potentiality locked into each human being. All Christians are to live by one and the same desire for the same goal. St. Gregory of Nyssa says that "there is only one vocation given to all those who believe in him...that is to be called Christians."[5]

Thus in the matter of perfection there is no distinction between men, women, and children healthy and sick, whether physically or psychically, rich or poor. St. John Chrysostom is clear on this point:

> The Holy Scriptures do not know any such distinction. They enjoin that all lead the life of the monk, even if they are married men who have children as Paul says (and when I say Paul, I say also Christ). He demands from them the same rigorous observance as that demanded from monks.[6]

Our whole fullness and perfection reside in an assimilation to the likeness of Christ. But it is not just Christ as a moral example outside of us, but Christ, the risen Lord, dynamically living in us and working in us through this grace of the indwelling Trinity. Grace for them is no longer a created entity. It is primarily an encounter with the living Trinity whose life is indwelling us and acting at all times to divinize us.

This relationship through Christ given to all human beings is called the "imageness" within it. This relationship was meant by God to become by the divining power of the Holy Spirit an experiential knowledge of being in union with the Lord Jesus and freely surrendering to obey his Word, his Logos, which he is speaking at all times. This potential union in Christ is locked in the potential imageness of each human person. Sin has distorted this call to be free in God's love, yet it can never be destroyed. This image resides in all human beings insofar as we possess an intellect and a will in our very natures. It can never be taken away. No matter how much a person may sin, this potential of being "toward" an intimate union with Christ, this imageness will always remain.

In the second century Irenaeus wrote, and Athanasius and all other Eastern Fathers repeated him, that God became man in order that all human beings would become God.[7] This was meant in a very real way, not that we ever become God by nature, but, as St. Peter says in his second epistle, we are called to be "participators in the divine nature" (2 Pet. 1:4). This is the great truth that the early Christians seized, and this is what made them so optimistic and so joyful in regard to God's created universe. In a pagan world where there was so much pessimism and fatalism, the non-Christians did not have a clear understanding of why they were living. But Christ truly came to give us this tremendous revelation: that God so loved us as to give us the possibility of becoming truly daughters and sons of God.

St. Irenaeus is the first great Father of the Church to develop this doctrine of the image and likeness in us human beings. As we have said, all human persons possesss the imageness insofar as they possess a body and an intellectual soul. This Irenaeus calls *imago in plasmate,* or the "frame" of a human person. Yet guided by Paul's teaching that the human being is to progress in perfection in Jesus Christ, "safe and blameless, spirit, soul and body" (1 Thess. 5:23), Irenaeus insists that a human being is not fully developed until the potential in the imageness of body and soul evolves through the Holy Spirit into the human spirit. We do not have a body and a soul and a spirit, as separable compartments. We are meant by God, as Jesus in his humanity evolved, to live fully on these various levels of body, soul, and spirit relationships. You can see that not all human beings live and die on this earth in the attainment of being in the likeness to Christ, or live on the spirit plane. The spirit is not present when a person is born. Yet for Paul and the early Fathers, the Spirit was considered as a gift of God's love bringing about our divinizing into Spirit-filled children of God. Some Christians enter into this spiritual relationship with the indwelling Christ, but they may lose this relationship to God's Spirit by sin.

This is a concept that is quite different from that found in Western philosophy. It is not considered in the Western thinking that human nature is incomplete without the whole person being guided by the indwelling Holy Spirit. The Holy Spirit is God's gift who brings about the perfecting of human nature. Irenaeus writes: "There are three things out of which, as I have shown, the complete person is composed — flesh [body], soul, and spirit."[8]

Where Do We Find the Image and the Likeness?

If we have been made by God-Trinity according to Christ's image and likeness, where, therefore, do we find this image and likeness in us? Is the image of God in us different from the likeness?

It is at this point that we might lose patience as we read the writings of the early Fathers. One writer may interpret "image" as the total, ontological, created human person in process of becoming ever more one's true self in a greater, conscious union with the incarnate Word, Jesus Christ, while he might see "likeness" as what we would call grace. It is in this openness of ourselves to the guidance of the Spirit of the risen Christ that we find the likeness that can increase as we respond in loving obedience to the Word incarnate or this relationship can decrease if we harden our hearts and turn away from such an intimate union with Christ.

In the fourth century, St. Epiphanius, a very outspoken person, said impatiently: "Where the image is and in what it consists, God alone knows, but we should admit the image [*kat' eikona*] in man lest we appear to reject God's gift and refuse to believe him."[9] But when we begin to examine the individual writings of these Fathers, especially of the Christian East, we find a seeming confusion. On one page they may write about the image as distinct from the likeness; on another page they write about the image becoming always brighter and brighter, or they may state that it was lost by sin or covered over by sin.

Actually there is no contradiction. The teaching on the image and likeness admits of very fluid concepts, and only from the context can one understand what the individual writer is trying to say. But by and large, there is among the Fathers the basic conviction of the spiritual life as a progressive development of the image and likeness from the very moment that we are born to the moment that we die, with this process of growing into greater oneness with the Trinity in and through Jesus Christ and the Holy Spirit continuing unendingly into the life to come.

One great richness coming out of this patristic teaching on image and likeness is the holistic emphasis on human nature. The total human person is created to progress in union with God-Trinity by living fully. We are not persons who have a body or who possess a soul or have a spirit. Rather we are persons who are "embodied beings" and "ensouled beings" and "enspirited" beings in vital interpersonal relationships on the various integrated levels of human existence with the indwelling Trinity. The early Fathers conceived "nature" as the total being, created as body and soul with the potential to respond through the Holy Spirit to become a spirited being in living consciously in the likeness of Christ. All this is embraced by the one general word *physis* (nature). *Physis* is a broader term than our term "nature." It embraces not only the nature of a human person as he or she comes from the hand of God, but it also looks toward its completion and is defined according to its fulfillment rather than the beginning stage.

Thus *physis* is everything that God puts into a human being, whether it is in the beginning stage or the final one, and it also includes that which comes to a person after he or she is baptized and begins to lead a virtuous life. The Fathers consider, therefore, everything in nature or that comes to nature after baptism as being "according to nature" (*kata physin*). All is within the structure of true human nature. There is nothing superimposed from the outside upon nature. The patristic doctrine emphasizes the idea of a dynamic drawing out of the potencies present in the first creation. The expression "supernature," to indicate what God creates and puts on top of nature like one story of a building built upon another, as in the scholastic phrase "grace builds on nature," is never used by the Fathers.

Sin according to the early Fathers is anything that is against human nature, which God creates as always very good. Anything that is "against nature" (*para physin*) has to come from outside. Everything in us that is given to us in our creation or that comes after is a drawing out of God's initial creation of human nature as good and always potentially being driven by God toward greater union with the triadic life.

We can lose created grace by breaking away from God's gift of sharing in his eternal life. Even if we do sin, our human nature can never be evil or corrupt, but remains always in the goodness of God's continued call to us to return to live fully unto God's glory. We may succumb to sin and commit moral evil, but such evil is not able to touch or destroy or corrupt our nature. We can lose grace, the divine likeness, but the human nature given to us by God is good and can never be destroyed.

The will, therefore, is the great determining factor. There are two parts in the human will. The first is self-possession, or the autonomy to determine our destiny (*autexousion*). This autonomy of free will can never be taken from us. We are always intrinsically called by God to be master of our own destiny. No outside agent coming in and touching us can ever force us against our will. We must determine freely in the face of all temptations to succumb or not.

There is another part of our human free will that the Fathers call *eleutheria*. It is that quality which we would perhaps call "integrated nature." You, as a total person, react according to your total nature for your total fulfillment as God has eternally wished you to respond to his freely given call to share his community of love. Possessing this type of true freedom, your whole being harmoniously reacts according to the powers which God has given you. In the first sin of Adam and Eve, human beings lost this true freedom, this harmony among all their powers, so that all the bodily appetites and senses along with the internal faculties of memory, emotions, understanding, imagination, and will tend toward their own proper end and unity, and intimate friendship with God is lost.

Irenaeus is the first of the early Fathers to give us an authentic Christology. He speaks of the incarnation as the necessary means to bring about the salvation that we human beings could never have attained by our own power. The Word of God became human in order that we might become God through God's graceful divine life. Christ had to become all things to us except sin. He comes as the perfect image of God, and he gives us the possibility of restoring the likeness of God in us, in our entire human being.

It is not merely our soul that becomes the temple of God, but our whole being must be refashioned "according to Christ." In the depths of our being, on body, soul, and spirit levels, we must become conscious sharers of his divine and human natures. In this teaching, Irenaeus and those writers who followed his holistic spirituality, nicely unite the mysticism of St. John and St. Paul. He identifies the flesh of Christ with ours and states that the promise of eternal life is given us because Christ is the Prince of life.

God Is Ever Calling Us

In a very summary fashion we have tried to present here the main lines of the patristic anthropology of our human nature, built around the image and likeness concept from Scripture. Hopefully we have seen that this doctrine flows directly from Scripture. In a very true sense, as God conceived us, we are truly human persons only when we emerge from ourselves and rediscover by God's grace our true selves. This means to turn to him, Jesus Christ, who is the perfect image of his Father.

I believe we can find in our daily modern life many applications of this doctrine of the image and likeness. It will certainly recover for us a more existential view of the life of God-Trinity personally working in all areas of our human nature, made up of body, soul, and spirit levels of relationships to God, to neighbor, and to the entire created world around us. We can also discover a more personalistic and dynamic view of grace as primarily God-Trinity, as uncreated energies of divine love in self-giving as Father, Son, and Spirit to us in each moment of our existence, as we will see in the chapter on uncreated energies.

God has created all human beings with a basic drive toward union with him. All human beings are desperately searching for happiness, but many do not know who it is who alone can ever satisfy this yearning. If we suppress this basic image and these drives given us by God for becoming sharers in his own divine trinitarian life, then our hearts will always remain restless until we rest in God himself.

With our emphasis today on more individual personalism, we are now more open to move away from a perfect but immutable, static God who is far away from us to discover from Scripture and the writings of the great Christian mystics of both East and West the humility of the pursuing Trinity that wishes to give themselves to us in every event of our human existence. Every moment is a constant "vocation" in which God is calling us to respond to his invitation to become more like his Son according to whose image and likeness we are being created as we cooperate in this process of divinization, of fructifying the seeds of the trinitarian life implanted within us in our creation and baptism.

We do not wait until heaven to aspire to this intimate union with the Trinity. We enjoy this divine life even now as we go through our daily lives, as we seek to put on the mind of Jesus by an inner revolution and strive to live according to his virtuous life. Our union with Christ can never be taken from us by any event, trial, cross, or person, not even by death itself (Rom. 8:35). This union as we live in the likeness of Christ spills outward into loving action. Contemplation and action blend together so that we really create, as Teilhard de Chardin has said, a divine milieu. Wherever we are, the whole universe is truly a temple of God, and we find God everywhere and in all things dynamically working to bring us and the whole universe to Christ. We are not alone; we are a part of this total cosmos. We find our completion precisely in our activities in this world done in and for and through Jesus Christ. We go to God together with this whole wonderful world of ours. The world must never become a hindrance, but rather an instrument through which we can respond to God, and, in listening to his call and accepting it, we can thus move ever more from being made according to God's image to become actuated in the very likeness of Christ.

CHAPTER THREE

Luminous Darkness: The Apophatic Way

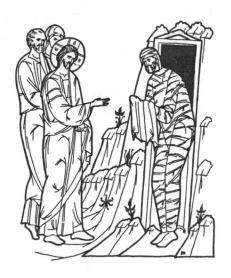

ERHAPS THE DISTINGUISHING CHARACTERISTIC of Eastern Christian mysticism is its *apophatic* quality. Similar to Far Eastern mysticism, Eastern Christian mysticism insists that the highest union, the infused union in which God speaks to us directly about himself, is not achieved in any conceptual knowledge, but in an immediate, experimental knowledge wherein he opens himself to us. We can never come to this knowledge through any mere rational concept, through any discursive method of our own. God, purely and simply and in his transcendence, reveals himself to us when and how he wishes to do so.

After years of our own preparation and cooperation through continued purification, God reveals himself to us. In utter humility before the awesome Source of all being, we are so open to his presence as to see him in everything and to see ourselves as "a participator of God's own nature" (2 Pet. 1:4).

A Knowing by Not Knowing

Against the heresy of Eunomius in the fourth century, the great Cappadocian theologians Basil, Gregory of Nazianzus, and Gregory of Nyssa developed an apophatic theology as a necessary corrective against Eunomius's teaching that the essence of God could be clearly known by us human beings. This is not merely the *via negationis* of St. Thomas Aquinas, who, with the Cappadocians and all other true Christian theologians down through the centuries, insists on a negative theology to correct the affirmative theology that attributes perfections to God. Such a method is necessary to correct the manner of speaking in human concepts which never can exhaust the infinite perfections found in God. Such a theology attempts to speak of God by what he is "not," rather than by what he is.

For the Cappadocians, God is superior to all other essences. The biblical description of God, the "One" who is, expresses the divinity that is infinite and above all not knowable on the part of finite creatures. God is the only truly authentic being that is opposed to all other nonbeing.

The "father" of Christian mysticism, St. Gregory of Nyssa, opened theology to the positive elements of the apophatic approach. He developed in his writings a mystical theology that would form the basis of that dialectical, mystical experience of God, a knowing, by not knowing, that Pseudo-Dionysius evolved and bequeathed to Maximus the Confessor, to Scotus Erigena, to the fourteenth-century Rhenish and Flemish mystics such as Meister Eckhart, Tauler, Suso, and Jan Ruysbroeck, and to the anonymous writer of the fourteenth-century English classic *The Cloud of Unknowing.*

Such a dialectical, mystical apophatic theology holds that the "not" is the beginning of a knowledge of God by experience. It is based on the impossibility of adequately defining God by human concepts, but not on the impossibility of somehow knowing him. Such an approach is based, not on an absolute no, but on a relative no, a *pas encore,* to quote the Russian theologian Cyprian Kern.[1]

This is a question of true theological knowledge, but it is more in the experience of God as giving himself to the repentant mystic who approaches God in a state of brokenness and interior poverty of spirit. Vladimir Lossky describes the knowledge of God beyond all conceptualization that Gregory of Nyssa called "theognosis," knowledge taught by God:

> Having failed to recognize the One it desires among the intelligible and incorporeal beings, and abandoning all that it finds, it recognizes the One it is seeking as the only One he does not comprehend.... Union with God is presented as a path which goes beyond vision and intelligence to the area where knowledge is suppressed and love alone remains — or rather, where *gnosis* becomes *agape.*[2]

We must note that the overwhelming infinity of God is nevertheless a presence of God as experienced by the contemplative. The modality of recognizing this presence is, however, a new and higher form of knowledge that surpasses the powers and experiences of human beings. Thus Gregory resorts to such paradoxical terms as "luminous darkness," "sober inebriation," etc. He describes this presence without seeing in his *Commentary on the Song of Songs:* "The Bride is surrounded with the divine night in which the Bridegroom comes near without showing himself... but by giving the soul a certain sense of his presence while fleeing from clear knowledge."[3]

Transcendence and Presence Meet

This is the positive dialectical side to the apophatic theology of the Eastern Christian Fathers. The Incomprehensible One is present and is experienced by the Christian. It is this very presence that is spoken of. It is that very transcendence that brings darkness to our human reasoning powers. The emphasis is not on our incapacity to know God, but rather on the overwhelming infinity of God that is nevertheless present.

Presence and transcendence are one in apophatic theology. In paradoxical fashion, the closer one gets to union with God, the more blinding God becomes. This is not a matter of our knowledge of God becoming more abstruse, but of the nature of God itself becoming more present as a gift of the Holy Spirit to the pure and humble of heart. That presence brings to us the realization of the absolute awesomeness of the goal of our earthly journey.

Gregory describes this as a going beyond oneself, as in ecstasy, a state similar to drunkenness, sleep, and even passion. He speaks of Abraham in ecstasy before the "God who transcends all knowable symbols."[4] Having purified himself and studied all that there was to know of the divine attributes (the *cataphatic,* or positive approach), Abraham finds faith in the transcendent God. It is this that is ecstasy:

> And so, after this ecstasy, which comes upon him as a result of these lofty visions, Abraham returned once more to his human frailty. I am, he admits, dust and ashes, mute, inert, incapable of explaining rationally the Godhead that my mind has seen.[5]

After purification and study, God comes to Abraham in faith, and this carries Abraham beyond himself in that he sees himself as nothing and inert. This ecstasy is really brought on from outside. Passivity is this strange activity. Purification and illumination do not bring on ecstasy, but rather faith alone makes possible the experience of God coming to Abraham. The coming of the vision is what makes Abraham realize that he is nothing before God. The incomprehensibility of God overawes and mutes the fleshly mind and senses.

It is especially in Gregory's *Life of Moses* that we have a full presentation of the soul's journey up the mountain to meet God in the darkness of unknowing. In this work, Gregory develops the meaning of darkness. Although it does mean that the Christian possesses an incapacity to know God intimately, it primarily means that God is absolute unfathomable, the fullness of being, and we can "understand" this only in the darkening of our controlled faculties of imagination and intellection.

Like Moses' ascent to Mount Sinai, the movement of the individual toward enlightenment begins in the darkness of sin. He sees a ray of light of God that beckons him to leave the foothills and start climbing upward. The higher states are degrees of his entrance into the darkness of God's incomprehensibility. Gregory states this in his work on the Canticle of Canticles:

> Our initial withdrawal from wrong and erroneous ideas of God is a transition from darkness to light. Next comes a closer awareness of hidden things, and by this the soul is guided through sense phenomena to the world of the invisible. And this awareness is a kind of cloud, which overshadows all appearances, and slowly guides and accustoms the soul to look toward what is hidden. Next the soul makes progress through all these stages and goes on higher, and as she leaves behind all that human nature can attain, she enters within the secret chamber of the divine knowledge and here she is cut off on all sides by the divine darkness. Now she leaves outside all that can be grasped by sense or by reason, and the only thing left for her contemplation is the invisible and the incomprehensible.[6]

It should be noted that for Gregory of Nyssa the movement is not from darkness to light solely, but it is a continued process from darkness to light and then to shadow and again to light.[7]

Epectasis: Love Always Growing

A key doctrine of Gregory of Nyssa regarding the apophatic dialectical movement from darkness to light, from absence to presence of God, from absolute transcendence of God to his immanence is what he calls *epectasis*. This means a "stretching out," an exceeding of one's level of attained love of God, based on Paul's statement: "I strain ahead for what is still to come" (Phil. 3:13). The love of God is a force in us human beings expanding our being and making us infinitely capable of possessing God in an unending process of greater and greater growth, both in this life through contemplation and also in the life to come. Gregory describes true perfection as "never to stop growing toward what is better and never to place any limit on perfection."[8]

The reasons he gives for this continued growth are first that Beauty, God himself, is infinite. The second is that the Beautiful is of such a nature that the desire for it can never be fully satisfied.[9] Gregory writes:

> The soul that looks up toward God and conceives that good desire for his eternal beauty constantly experiences an ever new yearning for that which lies ahead and her desire is never given its full satisfaction.[10]

This stretching forth to possess more and more the Unpossessable is described in antinomical terms. For Gregory, this unrest and the stretching forth to higher perfection and greater assimilation into the Absolute, this motion toward greater being, is the same as stability.[11] Motion for Gregory means more than moving from one stage of perfection to another. The very transcendence of God is the reason that perfection itself is constant motion. God is eternally at rest; yet he exists always in an outgoing motion of love to share himself with the other. Thus after the contemplative soul has been purified of all taint of self-absorption, God attracts it continually to:

... keep rising ever higher and higher, stretching with its desire for heavenly things to those that are ahead (Phil. 3:13),
as St. Paul tells us, and thus it will always continue to soar
ever higher... and thus the soul moves ceaselessly upwards
always reviving its tension for its onward flight by means of
the progress it has already realized. Indeed, it is only spiritual activity that nourishes its force by exercise; it does not
slacken its tension by action, but rather increases it.[12]

It was to the mysterious personage that history has called Dionysius the Areopagite that these insights of Gregory of Nyssa
would be handed down in the famous small treatise called *The
Mystical Theology*.[13] In this treatise, apophatic theology reaches
its peak in transforming theology into a contemplation of the
mysteries of revelation. Mystical theology is not a branch of theology dealing with the aspects of higher contemplation and hence
applicable only to a few gifted persons.

By placing the accent so completely on the unknowability of
God's essence without yielding to agnosticism (a refusal to allow
a real knowledge of God), by emphasizing a higher knowledge
attainable by human beings as a gift from God, the Eastern Fathers, whose doctrine Pseudo-Dionysius aptly summarizes, saw
theology never as abstract and working through concepts, but as
contemplative. It raises the mind to those realities which pass all
understanding. Lossky writes:

> It is not a question of suppressing the antinomy by adapting
> dogma to our understanding, but of a change of heart and
> mind enabling us to attain to the contemplation of the reality
> which reveals itself to us as it raises us to God, and unites us,
> according to our several capacities, to him.[14]

In a classical passage, Pseudo-Dionysius describes the mystical
side of true apophatic theology:

> Nevertheless, he [Moses] did not attain to the Presence of
> God himself; he saw not him (for he cannot be looked upon),

but the place where he dwells. And this I take to signify that the divinest and highest things seen by the eyes or contemplated by the mind are but the symbolical expressions of those that are immediately beneath him who is above all. Through these, his incomprehensible Presence is manifest upon those heights of his Holy Places; that then it breaks forth, even from that which is seen and that which sees, and plunges the mystic into the Darkness of Unknowing, when all perfection of understanding is excluded, and he is enwrapped in that which is altogether intangible and noumenal, being wholly absorbed in him, who is beyond all, and in none else (whether himself or another); and through the inactivity of all his reasoning powers is united by his highest faculty to him, who is wholly unknowable; thus by knowing nothing he knows that which is beyond his knowledge.[15]

A Living Theology

In a correct apophatic theology there is no opposition to *cataphatic,* or positive theology. It encourages a positive theology expressed through rational concepts, but it constantly tells positive theologians that the expressions used by them are not really the way such and such a perfection or relation exists in God. It stimulates them to open up to the mystery of a living contact with the immanent God, who comes in a living experience.

The apparent conflicts between a speculative theology and that of a more mystical, experiential nature are resolved or made "livable" in the Liturgy of the Church, the experiential drama of dogma that takes the faithful into the heart of mystery to meet the living God of Abraham, Isaac, and Jacob beyond any concepts. "No language knows how to praise you, O God, worthily and the mind, vaster than the world, becomes dizzy in celebrating you."[16]

Dogmatic, speculative theology can tell us the distinction between substance and accidents and work out for us a theory of transubstantiation, but it is only in the immediate experience of celebrating the Eucharist and in receiving the Bread of Life that we come into a resolution of the antinomies of how eternity and time can meet. We experience how divinity can be joined with humanity, how Jesus Christ is both true God and true man, eternally in glory and yet always coming into our lives to touch our human bodies with his glorious Body and Blood, how we are Church, with many members and yet each member uniquely loved by God. We wait for the full "eschaton" to come, and yet in the Eucharist it has begun.

For one who has experienced the living theology so present in the Byzantine Holy Week and Easter services, the reconciliation of cataphatic and apophatic theology is an experience that brings together antinomies. It allows us human beings to live in the power of such antinomies, which function at the heart of our most transcendent human experiences. On the vigil of Easter, when the church is flooded with lighted candles and the priest sings out, "Christ is risen! He is truly risen!" one experiences the new victory of Christ over death. The Christian can find it easier to believe also that the same "divinizing process" has already begun in his or her life and in the lives of those praying together.

Not only do we believe it to be possible, as when we recite the Nicene-Constantinopolitan Creed each Sunday, but we know it through experience, through a liturgical and ecclesiastical situation. "The God Man lies in sabbath repose and yet is risen. Creatures lament, the sun hides its rays, stars are lightless, but for us, this Sabbath is blessed among all since Christ sleeps, to arise on the third day."[17]

Clarifications of Apophatic Theology

There are several points that need to be stressed that can highlight the main characteristics of true apophatic theology that could have great impact on our theology today.

1. Apophatic theology does not of itself suffice, for it is merely a negation of the knowledge of beings and is not yet a knowledge of God.

2. The knowledge which the Christian has of God is religious and existential, not conceptual. "It is not to any formal criterion, defined by Aristotle, that one owes the knowledge that God is unknowable, but through a religious experience, which may be in part due to a true understanding of beings, but which equally constitutes a revelation of the living God."[18]

The existential ways in which one may "know" God are the keeping of his commandments and above all through prayer. "Prayer offers [this union]...being the link between the rational creature and God."[19]

3. Such knowledge, therefore, is not based on a split between the senses and the intellect, as in a Platonic view, but rather between the created and the uncreated. Gregory Palamas in the fourteenth century summarized the traditional orthodox teachings of the early Greek Fathers on apophatic experience of the incomprehensible God. He must be viewed as a holistic theologian who saw the imageness of God, not only in the human intellect, but in the whole person, made up of body, soul, and spirit relationships. He writes: "The word 'man' is not applied to either soul or body separately, but to both together, since together they have been created in the image of God."[20]

4. The knowledge of God which the Christian possesses in Christ is a direct vision, and not, as Palamas's adversary Barlaam and his followers held, a vision mediated by angels. Palamas, contrary to a teaching that seemingly was credited to Pseudo-Dionysius, namely, that angels mediated human knowledge of God, taught that the coming of Christ had inverted the natural order of the universe (in which angels served as mediators between human beings and God) and had substituted in its place a totally new hierarchy wherein human beings surpassed angels and had a direct vision of God in Christ.

5. This knowledge, finally, is no mere "symbolic" knowledge,

but a real knowledge of God as he is in himself. Against the "intellectual symbolism" which Barlaam held to explain the mediated knowledge that we have of God, Palamas held that God was present in Christ. He himself had broken down the separation between the "up there" and the "down here," and Christ had made it possible for God to be forever present in our material world. In Palamas's incarnational view of history, Christ himself was the symbol uniting us and God. It was Christ and his Holy Spirit who illumined the hesychastic mystic. Jesus Christ, for Palamas, is the "sacrament" of God making God present to us in a direct knowing and experiencing of God.

In chapter 5 we will turn to the divine energies whereby the Holy Trinity, Father, Son, and Spirit, touch us human beings and communicate themselves to us in a real, direct way that still preserves the unknowability of God in his essence. It is in Palamas's articulation of this dialectical antinomy that we can gain great insight for our modern theology. In our personalistic world of today we yearn to encounter God immediately, person-to-person, through a knowledge that is beyond all concepts. We have seen how Palamas and the other Greek Fathers maintained that God is in himself, in his "essence," unknowable and "nonparticipable," while at the same time God is in his manifestations or "energies" knowable to us. Archbishop Basil Krivoshein summarizes this apophatic approach to true experiential knowledge:

> The divine substance is incommunicable and yet is, in a certain sense, communicated; we partake of the nature of God and yet at the same time we do not partake of it at all. So we must maintain both [affirmations] and lay them down as the standard of piety.[21]

A Logos Mysticism

WOULD LIKE TO BEGIN this most important subject that is at the heart of Christianity by explaining a very provocative mural that dominates the wall behind the altar in the Newman Chapel of the University of California at Santa Barbara. The artist, Michael Dvortsak, bases his work on Teilhard de Chardin's belief, grounded in the writings of St. Paul, St. John, and the Eastern Fathers, that, since the Word became flesh and lived among us, "Christ invests himself organically with the very majesty of his universe."

The artist has sought to draw out in dramatic pictorial form the implications of the incarnation in language the students at a modern university would understand. In this mural Christ is depicted with arms outstretched in a crucified form. In a circular movement pouring down from one hand and up to the other are the vivid symbols of a living world, that of the inner space of the submicroscopic and that of outer space, of the macrocosm, of planets and galaxies and quasars.

Christ looks down with intense interest and spiritual concern toward every created atom. The artist stresses the unity of the whole created universe in Christ, who has taken on matter and is "inside" the universe, creating, developing, and divinizing it until all is brought back in glory to the Father. It is an artistic profession of the faith proclaimed by St. Paul: "for in him were created all things in heaven and on earth, everything visible and everything invisible" (Col. 1:16).

The whole life cycle is shown to come forth from Christ, through him and in him, starting with the individual unicell of life, to the union of sperm and ovum, to the formation of the human foetus. From the mountains and valleys, making up the human being's complicated inner physical world, to the planets and galaxies of outer space, all things sweep out and down in the shape of a human heart from the head of Christ, back up from the bottom through the figure of Christ.

The artist is showing us that God loves his creation. The world is full of vibrant energy, God's own active and loving concern through the incarnate Word, Jesus Christ. The Body of Christ is being formed by the matter of this universe as each atom is brought forth under the power of Christ. God loves the world that is of his making. It is good, and he is involved in the formation of its future. He is present in it as an inner force, making it evolve. He lives for it. He dies for it. There is hope for this wildly careening universe, because there is a principle of harmony at its center. This principle is Christ the Evolver, Christ the Logos.

We and the World Are Joined to Christ

Christ is the Word, the Logos, through whom God speaks to us, and in that Speech we have our being. The abyss between God and nothingness is spanned through the Logos. He is our raison d'être, the reason why we exist and why the whole world was created and given into our hands to make our awesome response to the Giver of life. We would always be incapable of uniting with God in order to reach our true meaningfulness and fulfillment, unless God gave himself to us. "God's love for us was revealed when God sent into the world his only Son, so that we could have life through him" (1 John 4:9). St. Paul clearly shows us the plan of God's creation: "We are God's work of art, created in Christ Jesus to live the good life as from the beginning he had meant us to live it" (Eph. 2:10).

The Eastern Fathers saw clearly and fought tenaciously to uphold the true hypostatic union of the Word of God, from all eternity one substantially with the Father, God from God, Light from Light, begotten not made, of one substance with the Father, as the Nicene-Constantinopolitan Councils decreed solemnly. When God's Logos assumed flesh, our humanity, when he took upon himself matter, as eternally ordained by God in the total plan of creation, we human beings and the whole material world were irrevocably assumed into that hypostatic union. As divinity and humanity were joined into one being "without confusion," as the Council of Chalcedon (451) described the hypostatic union, so by analogy we and the world are joined together with divinity without confusion, but in a unity of love.

As the human nature of Christ, living united with his divinity, will always remain his glorified humanity, so too this created world will come into its fullness precisely by entering into a conscious relationship of love with God. Christ is acting within the evolving process of this world to allow the world to be itself and to let each of us to become our true selves.

Regardless of whatever culturally conditioned theological or philosophical vehicle the Fathers employed in interpreting the Christian message, the mystics, universally and throughout the centuries of Christianity, have moved within the context of a dynamic and evolutionary process of the unfolding of the God–human beings–world relationship.

As we Christians are led progressively into the inner meaning of reality, we are not led away from the created world, but rather we are led into reverence and worship of God as present everywhere within the created world. The flowers, the trees, birds, animals, the beauties of each new season, the sun, moon, stars, the mountains, lakes, oceans, the whole world reveals to the contemplative the loving presence of the Trinity. The Trinity give themselves to us in their many gifts, and above all, in their uncreated energies of love whereby each person of the Trinity, united in one nature of love, gives himself to each of us human beings as a gift of our unique Father, Jesus Christ, our brother and savior, and the Holy Spirit as the hidden, kenotic, self-emptying, binding love between the Father and Son to us. God-Trinity is contemplated and experienced by us human beings as an almighty Transcendence that is the Source of all created life.

We move even deeper into reality when we adore the presence of God as the One who "contains" the created world, gives it its "consistency." As Paul preached to the Athenians, our God "is not far from any of us, since it is in him that we live and move and exist" (Acts 17:28). We are not alone on this planet Earth. God is everywhere, present and holding up all of existence.

The Fourth Dimension through the Logos

The Eastern Fathers theologized from Scripture and from their lived mystical experiences. Filled with the Holy Spirit, they could equally move from a study of human beings made according to God's image and likeness to the events in all creation, to the study of Holy Scripture through various levels of God's revealing presence and loving activities.

The Eastern Fathers, because they were mystics, had the ability to view the history of salvation from the unified perspective of the Trinity. They could transplant themselves to a higher vantage point and could view the continuity of events from the first creation through the Old Testament to the New Testament to their own time in the light of the all-encompassing present moment, the ever *now* of God. Though they knew they were situated in the time that unfolded after the historical person, the Logos incarnate, had already come to earth, they also knew that they were in the present moment as regards God's eternal love. They were dominated by this eternal act of love that is always permanent, always constant, yet always being manifested in diverse creative moments.

The Fathers always saw the same Trinity unfolding their eternal love for us in an area that is out of space and time, although it is unfolding within the historical categories of our space and time. I like to call this the fourth dimensional perspective of the early Fathers. They were able to see the trinitarian activities ever operating in history, bringing about their eternal plan as conceived according to the divine Logos, whom the Father is eternally speaking and in whom, through whom, and with whom all things are being brought forth. This is the dynamic vision found in St. John's Gospel. The Logos is always operating in the universe to bring us into sharing the glory of God. This is Paul's vision of the whole world unfolding gradually into a new creation:

And for anyone who is in Christ, there is a new creation; the old creation has gone, and now the new one is here. It is all God's work. It was God who reconciled us to himself through Christ and gave us the work of handing on this reconciliation. (2 Cor. 5:17–18)

The Logos and the Logoi

The Fathers' doctrine of the Logos evidently comes from the teaching of John's Gospel. Before John had formulated his doctrine of the Logos made flesh, the Greeks had various philosophical interpretations of the term, but fundamentally the *logos* meant "not only the side of God which is reflected in creation, which touches the finite world; it is the ultimate reason which explains all existence, the eternal principle that underlies phenomena."[1]

In the Sapiential Books of the Old Testament, the Logos was the creating Word of God by which he "spoke, and they were made, he gave his command, and their frame was fashioned" (Ps. 32:9).

But John's Gospel gives a totally new revelation of Logos theology. For John, the Logos is the very principle of all that is and all that lives. It is found in each created thing and yet it is distinct from the creature. This principle hides within the depths of God. This is Yahweh's *Dabar* that he eternally speaks. It lies within God from eternity and is itself God.

> In the beginning was the Word;
> the Word was with God
> and the Word was God.
> He was with God in the beginning.
> Through him all things came to be,
> not one thing had its being but through him.
> All that came to be had life in him
> and that life was the light of men. (John 1:1–3)

This Logos, God, Life, Light, becomes a human being like us. He identifies with us in order that he may lead us out of darkness into the true Light, into a sharing with his very being, which is one with the glory, the Shekinah, of the awesome Godhead. This preexistent Word of God, God himself, is the meaning of the universe that existed before it was created. He becomes the model, the pattern by which the world is made. He is also the power that generates the world into being, especially the power that begets us human beings into his fullness as participators of his own glory, that of his Father, by making us children of the same Father.

Maximus the Confessor: A Logos Mystic

Of all the Church Fathers, Maximus the Confessor (d. 662) gives us the most complete vision of a Logos mysticism, summarizing and perfecting all that Origen, Athanasius, and his other predecessors had written on this point. For Maximus as for St. John, the whole world is interrelated in its harmony according to the differentiated *logoi* or the created existences of individual things according to the mind of God. All things are created through the Logos through whom the creative will of the Father flows.

The *logos* in each being is the principle of existence which relates a given creature to God as its cause. It also denotes the created existence of a thing founded in God's will that it should have existence. It is the principle of a coming-to-be and implies a participation in God as being. These *logoi* preexist in God and are contained in the Logos, the second person of the Trinity, who is the first principle and final end of all created things.[2]

It should be noted, as Polycarp Sherwood points out in citing Maximus's concept of the *logoi,* that these are in the mind of God, not as "inert models, but the very creative power of God, realizing itself in the creature."[3]

Hence we see a very dynamic vision of a world united in the mind of God, of a world of ideal *logoi* in process of being attained as the existential *logoi* in creatures move to completion under the power of the Logos, Jesus Christ. Inanimate objects have to exist according to their God-given *logoi*. They have no choice. But we human beings are made according to the image and likeness of God and are called by God to be cocreators of this entire universe. We possess free will — the ability to live consciously ac-

cording to the unique *logos* in each of us, by fulfilling, in union
with God's activity (grace), this inner principle of harmony and
order. If we do not choose to live consciously, we automatically
reject doing so.

For Maximus, the truly real human beings are those of us who
live according to the unique *logos* in each of us. This true *logos*
that makes us unique and individually our own true self is modeled on a conscious relationship in loving submission to the Logos
living within us and bringing forth our potencies to be, each of us,
a unique child of God, a conscious reflection of God's beauty and
perfection, but in being a human being, living fully unto God's
eternal glory.

Christ is the perfect Logos made human, the full image of the
unseen God (Col. 1:15), who most perfectly reflects the mind of
God. We have our total being insofar as we have a conscious, loving relationship to Christ, allowing him to fulfill within us that
imageness destined to be brought to perfection in our first creation by the potency God has given us. This image or *logos* is
to be actuated by a lifetime of knowledge and virtue that will
continue to expand in the life to come. The "unnatural" person does not live according to her or his *logos*, but according to
the principle of the *Alogos*, the Evil One, whose principle is not
self-sacrificing love, but rather *philautia*, or self-love.

For Maximus the great force which accomplishes self-mastery,
detachment, and harmonization of our human faculties according to our human nature is love. "Love, the divine gift, perfects
human nature until it makes it appear in unity and identity by
grace with the divine nature," says Maximus.[4]

Charity is not only the highest virtue, as St. Paul insists in
1 Corinthians 13, but it is the reality which embraces all, the link
with the world of God's uncreated energies of grace. It is the force
that united those that are differentiated. Love brings about the
union of the Word and human nature, the union of the personal
energies which egoism, or self-love, has dispersed. It effects union
among all human beings.[5]

The sacraments open us to God's grace to effect this unity, first in us, then through our reconciling work with the Holy Spirit in the universe. Especially baptism and the Eucharist are the sacraments wherein the divinization power of Christ and his Holy Spirit works most effectively in us. The Church is also a place of encountering Christ's divinizing grace. The Church is a microcosm of what can be accomplished by God's grace throughout the entire human race and the created cosmos. Both now in the Church and then in the whole world all distinctions will remain and yet, paradoxically, will be transformed. Maximus describes this synthetic union:

> Men, women and children profoundly divided as to race, nature, language, manner of life, work, knowledge, honor, fortune...the Church recreates all of them in the Spirit. To all she equally communicates a divine aspect. All receive from her a unique nature which cannot be broken asunder, a nature which no longer permits one henceforth to take into consideration the many and profound differences which are their lot.[6]

Maximus sees the operation of the Holy Spirit as taking place especially in the sacraments and in unceasing prayer. In every phase of one's spiritual development into a greater likeness to Jesus Christ, the Spirit is active. For Maximus, the Holy Spirit is at work in our purification accomplished through fear, reverence, and knowledge. The Spirit illumines the *logoi* of things and gives knowledge of the inner relationship of all things to Christ. It is the Spirit who bestows perfection through simple wisdom on those worthy of divinization.[7]

The Holy Spirit, as conceived by the Eastern Fathers, is the agent who divinizes, the one who sanctifies us. By his indwelling within us as in his temple, he makes the divine life present in us grow continuously. His work is to reveal and make present Jesus Christ, the Logos, within us and in all the world. The Spirit leads us to experience God as Father, Abba. He brings the Trinity to

our consciousness. Hence through the Spirit we are able to pray
unceasingly (Rom. 8:26–27) according to the ideal of the early
ascetics of the desert and the ideal of all Christians.

Immersed in Divine Fire

The Holy Spirit comes to us and creates us with our free cooperation into divinized beings, permeated by the divine trinitarian
energies working and loving within us. But it is in and through
the Logos made flesh, Jesus Christ, that we have the amazing as-
surance that our assimilation into the Godhead makes it possible
that we enter into our true uniqueness. This comes about, not by
absorption, but by the love we experience in the Father through
the Son in his Spirit and by the love we then have for each person
and creature made by God in and through that Logos.

In every mysticism the experience of the Absolute becomes
more unified and less diffused. The separation is of the false ego.
The union takes place between the true *I* and its being in the
Other, who is ultimate and has no second. But the Spirit of Jesus
makes it possible for the Christian mystic to become aware of her-
or himself, not as a subject, adoring a divine object, but as the *I*,
aware of itself as a child of God, a divinized being participating,
as St. Peter writes, in the very divine nature (2 Pet. 1:4) while
never losing the human nature. Such mystics gradually become
more and more aware of this trinitarian loving presence within
them at the core of their very being. In the depths of our being
the triune community dwells and actively loves us. It is here that
we find the self-giving of the unique personhood of the Father
and the Son and the Holy Spirit.

To describe this union, Maximus and so many other Eastern
Christian mystics have used the analogy of iron and fire.[8] The
iron and fire are found together in a fiery sword, but the piece
of iron effects exactly that which is in accordance with its own
nature. It glows as fire, but in a way that is proper to iron. The

glowing sword cuts and burns at the same time; as iron it cuts, as fire it burns.[9]

We Christians are given this incredible privilege by faith of actually being immersed into the fire of the Logos, both in deep, contemplative prayer and in the Eucharist, which cannot really be separated as two distinct moments of loving adoration. Yet the Logos incarnated does not come to us alone. He is, by his essence as Logos, relational. He points to and unveils the Father as he points from and images the Father to us. "I am in the Father and the Father in me" (John 14:10). Where Christ, the divine Son, is, there also is the Father and the Holy Spirit. "He that sent me is with me and he has not left me alone.... The Father abides in me" (John 13:29; 14:10). Where the Father and Son are present, there also is the binding love of the Holy Spirit, who loves the Father and the Son within us and with us.

The three persons do not remain inactive within the contemplative. Within us the Father utters his Word. He generates his Son, who is perfectly the image of his Father, the divine Logos, by a perfect response of love, which, with the love of the Father for the Son, breathes forth the Holy Spirit.

The Logos not only brings about this trinitarian union by his presence, but, by his activity within us, he speaks to us of the Father. The Holy Spirit loves the Father and the Son within us and with us. Christ teaches us to realize his love as Logos for his Father. He teaches us about the Father and the Holy Spirit, but he also associates his activities as Son with our potency to respond likewise in union with him to a similar act of filial relationship on our part with the Father. He teaches us how to adore, praise, love, and surrender ourselves of every element that is an obstacle to true filiation in God by repeating within us: "Behold, I come to do your will." He asks the Father that we be admitted into the mystery of divine love. "Father, I pray for them also ... that they may be one in us" (John 17:20). He demands of the Father and obtains our participation in his filial surrender of himself to the Father. "Father, may the love wherewith you have loved me be in them" (John 17:26).

Conclusion

We end with the beginning: Jesus Christ, the Alpha and Omega, the image of the Father according to whose image we have been created in potency to be contemplatives of that Logos, to become "children of God and coheirs of heaven," as Paul said (Rom. 8:17). Through a more intense, expanded consciousness of the transcendent presence of the Trinity, living and acting in all material creatures out of love for us, we too can enter into a more vivid act of faith in that trinitarian life living within us and loving us. The sense-phenomenal world will be a true symbol to such contemplatives. Not only will it point out to us the presence of the Trinity, but also the material world will effect what it stands for. The material world will be the point of a personal encounter, effecting a true union with a Father loving us as he loves his only begotten Son, with the Son loving his Father in union with us, the newly divinized children of God. This is brought about, not by nature, but by his uncreated energies, his grace, in union with the Holy Spirit, the bond of mutual love between the Father and his Son and his adopted children.

CHAPTER FIVE

God's Uncreated Energies of Love

ASTERN CHRISTIAN THEOLOGIANS developed the distinction between the divine essence and God's uncreated energies. This distinction is a means of explaining how God's being is unknowable to us in his essence, and yet God does truly communicate himself to us in a new knowledge and a new participation through his uncreated energies. The *energies* are God's mode of existing in relationship to his created world, especially to us. Such a distinction is not often made use of in Western Christianity, where God also is believed to be absolute and essentially unknowable in his divine nature. Nevertheless, he does relate himself to the created order and so is knowable to us through his uncreated energies of love.

Eastern Christian theologians from earliest times appealed to Holy Scripture to substantiate their claims for the distinction between God's essence and his energies. They appeal to Habakkuk to describe God's glory, brightness, light, rays, and power that are manifested to human beings:

> Eloah is coming from Teman,
> and the Holy One from Mount Paran.
> His majesty veils the heavens,
> the earth is filled with his glory.
> His brightness is like the day,
> rays flash from his hands,
> that is where his power lies hidden. (Hab. 3:3–4)

Other references in Scripture are quoted (e.g., Ps. 36:9; Gen. 17:22–23; 1 Tim. 6:16 and 2 Pet. 1:4). The Logos is spoken of by the early Fathers as the divine idea and energy, showing itself in creation. As has been pointed out, the Cappadocian Fathers, Basil, Gregory of Nazianzus, and Gregory of Nyssa, in their polemical writings against the Eunomians, wrote a great deal in an attempt to maintain the absolute transcendence of the unknowable essence of God and also the relationships of God to his creatures.

In their writings, the origin of their doctrine on the energies of God is evidently trinitarian. In defense of the mystery of the Trinity and in their elucidation of it, these Cappadocians insisted on the distinction between the divine essence and the energies. Jesus Christ (against Eunomius, who denied his divinity) and the Holy Spirit truly are a part of the divine essence. All three, having a common nature, produce identical divine energies *ad extra,* outside of the trinitarian nature of the one Godhead.

St. Basil shows how the unapproachable and unknowable essence of God can be, however, experienced through the energies of the divine nature:

If it were possible to contemplate the divine nature itself and find out what is proper to it and what is foreign through what appears, we would be in no need at all of words or other signs for the comprehension of what is sought. But because it is higher than the understanding of the things sought, and we reason, parting from certain signs about things that evade our memory, it is of all necessity that we be conducted by the *energies* to the research of the divine nature.[1]

Basil also says: "For his [God's] energies descend down to us while his essence remains inaccessible."[2]

St. Gregory of Nazianzus, the theologian who greatly influenced the thinking of Gregory Palamas, wrote less in the context of polemics than the other two Cappadocians did and gave us a clearer doctrine of the energies of God. In using the image of Moses going up to Mount Sinai and being clothed in the cloud, Gregory writes:

I was running, as if to seize God, and thus I ascended to the mountain, and penetrated the cloud. Having got inside far from matter and material things, I gathered up into myself, as much as possible. And when I looked, with difficulty, I saw the backside of God, and this while concealed in the stone, in the Word Incarnate for our cause; and looking a little further on, not upon the first and pure nature known to itself, I mean to the Trinity and that which lies inside the first veil and is concealed by the Cherubim, but the last one, which reaches us.[3]

Here is the basis for the favorite image of the sun emitting its rays to the earth used by Gregory of Nyssa, which would be repeated by all the succeeding Eastern theologians, especially by Palamas:

As the sun, according to the divine dispensation, tempering the vigor and sincerity of its rays by the intermediate air, emits to those receiving it a proportionate splendor and heat, remaining by itself unapproachable to the weakness of our nature, thus also the divine power, by a similarity to the given example, infinitely surpassing our nature and inaccessible to participation... gives to the human nature what is in her power to receive.[4]

The Forthgoing of God

What Palamas would simply call "energy," Pseudo-Dionysius would call by various attributes, showing how God goes forth toward his created world to share his being or unlimited perfections. Some of the Areopagite's expressions indicating God's energies are the following: God's "forthgoing" (*proodos*) or manifestations of light, moved by the Father,[5] the "manifestation" of God, given harmoniously,[6] the divine "illumination," or the "ray" of God (*aktina*) or the "supersubstantial ray,"[7] and finally, the "distribution" (*metadosis*).

With such language Pseudo-Dionysius preserves the distinction between God's simplicity in essence and his "manifestations" in sharing his being in uncreated love toward us human beings and the created world. This is clearly seen in his statement: "Providence and goodness are participated in by human beings, which gifts go forth from God who is in his essence outside all participation yet overflowing with liberal profusion in his uncreated energies."[8]

The end of our human lives is to attain "mystical knowledge," the summit of God's sharing himself with us. Here we see Dionysius's understanding that God's energetic action toward us is completely gratuitous on his part. It is not we who raise ourselves to such a state, but God's freely given energies which work in us. We must offer no obstacle to this action. In one of the most famous passages in the Dionysian corpus, we see how holy minds come to enjoy a union devoid of confusion, yet enter into a true participation with God's action as illuminator:

> Leave behind the sense and the operations of the intellect, and all things sensible and intellectual, and all things in the world of being and nonbeing, that thou mayest arise, by unknowing, toward the union, as far as is attainable, with him who transcends all being and all knowledge. For by the unceasing and absolute renunciation of thyself and of all things, thou mayest be borne on high, through pure and entire self-abnegation, into the superessential Radiance of the Divine Darkness.[9]

This union by participation is a mystery. How can God share his being with us human beings in such a way that we really participate in God's divinity without at the same time becoming God? This is the mystery of *theosis,* the divinization process of grace whereby the Christian is brought into a loving union with God through the divine energies, and still God retains his complete superessential being. Part of this mystery of how individual human persons do really experience the full divinity and yet each person experiences God in his energies according to different proportions is stated by Dionysius: "It is all the divinity completely which is participated by each participator, and by none in any part."[10]

To maintain such an antinomy Dionysius gives us a principle repeated often by Palamas whenever he seeks to reconcile apparent contradictions, at least that which seems to be such to the human mind: "Divine things should be understood in a God-fitting manner."[11] It is this which theologians must ever keep in mind that alone will resolve all apparent contradictions and justify all antinomies in divine things.

No distinction humanly made can adequately describe the distinction between God's simplicity and essence and his participable self-giving in his energies. Let us look more closely at the system that Gregory Palamas developed from the writings of the

Greek Fathers as mentioned above, especially from the writings of Gregory of Nazianzus and Pseudo-Dionysius.

Participation in God's Life

We have already pointed out how Gregory Palamas insisted with all his predecessors on the unknowability of God in regard to his essence. Yet he strongly asserts that we do indeed know and participate in God through Christ. "But there is one fact which stands distinct with reference to this transcendence: the complete and unadulterated existence in us of Jesus."[12]

We are at the crucial node of Palamas's thought when we approach the question of the knowability and participability of God in and through his energies. The intensity of his concern for this problem of the possibility of the Christian's having a share in God's nature by participation in his energies is shown by the vigorous manner in which he tackles the question:

> Since a human person can participate in God and since the superessential essence of God is absolutely unparticipable, there is a certain something between the unparticipable essence and the participants which permits them to participate in God. And if you suppress that which is between the unparticipable God and the participants ... oh, what a void! — you separate us from God by destroying the bond and establishing a great uncrossable abyss between God on the one hand and creation and the governing of creatures on the other.
>
> We must then seek another God who possesses not only his own proper end within himself, his own proper energy and his own proper Godhead, but one who is a good God — for thus it will no longer suffice for him to exist only for the contemplation of himself — not only perfect, but surpassing all fullness; thus, in effect, when, in his goodness, he will

wish to do good, he will be able to do it; he will be not only immobile, but he will put himself into motion; he will thus be present for all with his manifestations and his creative and providential energies; in a word, we must seek a God in whom we can have a share in one way or another, so that by participating in him, each one of us may receive, in the manner proper to him and according to the analogy of participation, being, life and deification.[13]

Every "essence" has to have an "energy" if it is to be more than merely "possible." Palamas combined both meanings and applied the term to God's manifestations in the created order: God has real existence in the world insofar as he is manifested to the world. This is another way of saying that God has real existence in the world insofar as he creates the world, i.e., gives it existence by giving it a share in his own real existence in and through the "energies."

The energies are manifestations of God. Still, even though they are many and diverse, they are *one* in God. Hence God's simplicity is maintained, but not at the price of isolating him from contact with his creation. These manifestations are "God coming forth" — God insofar as he does not hide in his unknowable essence, but shows himself to us human beings.[14]

Palamas, as has been said above, works out a doctrine of God's essence and his uncreated energies in order to preserve the basic truth of Christian revelation, that we human beings have been in God's eternal act of love ordered to participate in his very own being.

For Eastern Christian thought, the energies signify an exterior manifestation of the Trinity. God is not determined by any of his attributes and all determinations are logically posterior to his essence. When God is described as love, life, truth, etc., we understand the energies as subsequent to the very being of the Trinity.

The doctrine of the energies, as distinct from the essence, is the basis of all mystical experience. God, who is inaccessible in his essence, is present in his energies "as a mirror," according to Palamas's saying, remaining invisible in that which he is. He is wholly unknowable in his essence, yet he is revealed in his energies.

This doctrine makes it possible to understand how the Trinity can remain incommunicable in essence, and yet dwell within us according to the promise of Christ. When one receives the deifying energies, one receives the indwelling of the Holy Trinity, which is inseparable from its natural energies. The distinction made between the essence and energies makes it possible to preserve the real meaning of the words "partakers of the divine nature" (2 Pet. 1:4).

In the divinization process, we are by grace made participators of what God is by nature, except that we remain creatures. St. Symeon the New Theologian (d. 1022) insists in his writings, which greatly influenced Palamas, that we are made gods by participation, by grace.[15]

The energies of God are uncreated divine activity. The divine essence, as has been said repeatedly, is inaccessible to us human beings. God, however, does communicate himself. He can be known experientially and we can reach him in true union or divinization. Palamas's distinction between the essence of God and the energies or divine operations which are forces proper to and inseparable from God's essence in which he goes forth from himself, manifests and communicates himself, is a recognition of the fact that God is both totally inaccessible and at the same time accessible.

We must open ourselves to God's uncreated energies that are always "gracing" us at every moment in each event. This is the mystery of the *synergy* (a working together) that the Eastern Fathers stressed in their development of *praxis,* or the ascetical life. We may be tainted by sin and our fallen state inherited from our ancestors, yet we have freedom locked within our consciousness. We can rise and go back to our Father in a *metanoia,* in a conversion and surrender of ourselves to God. When we do cooperate, the result is a divine state produced within our inner being. "It is when you have in your soul the divine state that you really possess God within yourself; and the true divine state is love toward God, and it survives only by practice of the divine commandments."[16]

Divinized through Energies

We are divinized and reach our fulfillment of being a child of God through the divine energies or grace. "God in his completeness deifies those who are worthy by uniting himself with them, not through the hypostasis — that belonged to Christ alone — not through the essence, but through the uncreated energies."[17] Thus, although Palamas uses the term "grace" with the same flexibility and richness as did the other Greek Fathers, his primary definition of grace would probably be: God, pouring himself out to us by his divine energies in order that he might unite us with him by making us true children of God.

The primary meaning of grace (which admits of an infinity of growth) centers around God's energetic process of divinizing us into the very likeness of Jesus Christ, the image of the Father and yet the image according to whom we have all been created.

> This process of purification and sanctification through which we grow in participating in the nature of the trinitarian life admits of a continual growth unto infinity. The very nature of grace as God's trinitarian life within us presupposes continued growth. To accept the divine energies as grace, therefore, is to accept the necessity of constantly moving toward the Trinity. Gregory of Nyssa wrote: "The grace of the Holy Spirit is given to everyone with the understanding that there is to be an augmenting and increase of what is received."[18]

Palamas's holistic approach is refreshing in the light of biblical research and modern theological approaches to an incarnational view of grace as God-for-us humans in all relationships, not merely God toward a human being as a mind. We are, therefore, according to Palamas, made according to God's image and likeness precisely in our entire make-up: body, soul, and spirit. In our total openness to God in his "graceful" energies on all our levels of being, we fulfill the image and likeness as the crown of all God's works, as the rulers and faithful stewards of the cosmos.

Because we are opened to God's grace on all levels, including our bodily relationships to God and the cosmos, we are considered by Palamas as superior even to the angels:

> Whereas the angels are appointed to serve the Creator and have as their only mission to be under authority (it is not being given to them to rule over inferior beings unless they are sent to do this by the Preserver of all things), we are preordained, not only to be ruled, but to rule over all that which is on the earth.[19]

If God's grace operates also on body relationships, then the body also can experience repercussions of God's activities. This is precisely what Palamas insisted upon as he defended the ancient Eastern Christian form of mysticism called *hesychasm,* with its holistic approach to prayer, including the use of bodily postures and breathing techniques to aid the contemplative to meet the indwelling Trinity in the deification process.

Hesychasm is a form of Eastern Christian mysticism that has its roots in the spirituality of the Fathers of the desert, especially that which developed from the Macarian school of the heart, as further developed on Mount Sinai and in the fourteenth century on Mount Athos. It places great stress on ascetical practices and an interior attentiveness in controlling the movements of the "heart" so as to reach a state of inner tranquility called *hesychia,* which in Greek means rest or tranquility. With all of our human being integrated, body, soul, and spirit, we are able to be attentive to God's commands and wishes as we become freed and integrated by the divinizing power of the Holy Spirit to do always what most pleases God.

The Taboric Light

Christ always shone during his earthly life with the trinitarian energy, the Taboric light, yet generally it remained invisible for most persons who saw him. The Transfiguration was not a phenomenon limited in time and space. No change took place at the moment as far as Christ was concerned, not even in his human nature, but a change took place in the consciousness of the three apostles, who suddenly for some measure of limited time had the ability to see the Master as he was, always resplendent in eternal light. The Holy Spirit remains invisible to us, yet is constantly manifesting himself in light through his sanctifying, deifying powers.

We become divinized as we become filled with the light of Tabor of the Holy Spirit in the degree that we make ourselves open to what is always present in the trinitarian, uncreated energies through asceticism. Divinization is not a one-sided act of God but rather an intimate, personalized relationship between the human individual and the trinitarian persons. This is brought through a mutual cooperation between God and us human beings. The goal of the ascetical life is not to deaden the bodily passions, but rather to dispose ourselves to acquire God's gift of a new energy which will allow both body and mind to share in the life of God's divinizing grace.

As we have said above, the Fathers made the distinction between the knowable and unknowable in God that seems somehow to be overcome in the mystical union that is called "deification" by grace in which "man transcends his nature. Being mortal, he become immortal; being corruptible, he becomes incorruptible; having a short life, he receives life eternal; being man, he becomes God," as Gregory of Nyssa wrote.[20]

It is Jesus Christ alone who has united divinity and humanity in his *hypostasis,* or one-personhood. Thus in his glorified human-divine life he communicates to all baptized in his name the Divine Energy or Sanctifying Grace. For Palamas, there is no other grace worthy of the name; all else is natural. The glorified hypostasis of Christ becomes prolonged through his Church. Thus Christ becomes the divine and uncreated life of the individual Christian. The Church is a real, visible, divinized community. One member living in Christ lives also with one's fellow Christians in whom Christ also lives.

Palamas insists upon a true knowledge of God in his energies: "He who contemplates God, not through the medium of a foreign symbol, but through a natural symbol, has seen God."[21]

In Palamas's use of the Taboric light as a symbol of the highest transforming power of the trinitarian energies working on the whole human person we can see his reliance on the writings of Symeon the New Theologian. Both Palamas and Symeon taught that such an immersion into the trinitarian life admits of ecstatic moments in which God is seen as brilliant light within the human darkness. The two areas, although separate, namely, God's ineffable beauty and glory and our sinfulness that still needs healing, coexist in such an experience, as we read in one of Symeon's mystical hymns:

> But, O what intoxication of light, O what movements of fire!
> O what swirlings of the flame in me, miserable one that I am,
> coming from you and your glory!
> The glory I know it and I say it is your Holy Spirit,
> who has the same nature with you and the same honor,
>   O Word; ...
> I thank you that you have made me worthy to know,
> however little it may be,
> the power of your divinity.
> I thank you that you, even when I was sitting in darkness,
> revealed yourself to me, you enlightened me,

you granted me to see the light of your countenance that is
   unbearable to all....
You appeared as light, illuminating me completely from your
   total light.
And I became light in the night, I was found in the midst of
   darkness.
Neither the darkness extinguished your light completely,
nor did the light dissipate the visible darkness,
but they were together, yet completely separate,
without confusion, far from each other, surely, not at all
   mixed.
So I am in the light, yet I am found in the middle of the
   darkness.
So I am in the darkness, yet still I am in the middle of the
   light.[22]

For the Eastern Christian mystics there was a real vision of
the Taboric light that occurred at various times, dependent upon
one's growth in compunction and humility. But even when the
vision of such a light was not present, the light presence of the
Trinity still shone in the strong, spiritual awareness of the indwelling Trinity. It is a contemplation that allows the intelligence
to remain completely simple, totally integrated into God, stripped
of all thoughts and bathed in the light of God. Symeon describes
this inner light:

> The intelligence cannot find any other object, but the light
> on which it has been fixed....It rests then in the abyss of
> the divine light which allows it to perceive nothing outside
> of itself. Indeed, this is what is meant: "God is light" and
> the supreme light. For those who reach this, it is the repose
> of all contemplation.[23]

Such a light to the intellect is a prelude to the full glory that
awaits Christians in their total transformation into Christ. This is
what fills Christians with perpetual joy and drives out all passion-

ate, disturbing thoughts and gives them the vision, even now, that the Savior in the Sermon on the Mount promised when he said: "Blessed are the pure of heart, for they shall *see* God" (Matt. 5:8).

We progressively become more transformed through the knowledge and contemplative experience of knowing God and of being known and loved by him. Jesus Christ renders us already through his Spirit to be risen from the dead. He vivifies us and gives himself to us in the most intimate union that will know no end of growth.

Such is the meaning of the ultimate stages of theology in which the contemplative, purified of all self-love, enters into a living relationship of continued communion with the Holy Trinity. We receive knowledge in the most apophatic sense: knowledge not by our own knowing, but knowledge infused by a mystical union with the indwelling Trinity.

In a word, to be invaded by God is to allow God to invade the world by our being present to him, who is everywhere present as loving, personalized, uncreated energies of love. It is to become so emptied of our nothingness and sinfulness that the Trinity may pour out its richness of life upon the whole world through our intimate union with the Trinity. It is not only to find the Trinity living within us, but it is to make the world around us present to that same immanently present and loving Trinity.

CHAPTER SIX

Paradise Lost

E HAVE ALREADY SEEN, especially in chapter 4, that God created the first man and woman "according to his own
image and likeness" (Gen. 1:26–27). The human person,
in having a body and a soul, possesses a nature that is a potential
to be completed from "imageness" into "likeness." This is done
by bringing our human nature into a steady growth as we make
free choices to live according to the indwelling Trinity. Thus we
live more fully "according to God's own likeness" by cooperating
as a whole person in loving submission to God's Holy Spirit.

Vladimir Lossky, a modern Russian Orthodox theologian, well describes God's plan whereby human beings would cooperate by making free choices out of love freely given back to God:

> Adam was to emerge from an infantile awareness by agreeing, through love, to obey God.... "Do not eat...." "Do not touch...." It is the very possibility of a really conscious love, of an ever-growing love that would take man away from an autonomous enjoyment not of one tree, but of all trees, not of one fruit, but of all that is sensible, to consume him, and all the universe with him, in enjoyment of God alone.[1]

The Fall

St. Basil knows what happens when we disobey God. Possessing a mind that can know good and a will to do it freely, we also possess in that same intellectual freedom "the faculty of turning away from the good."[2] We cannot accuse God of having acted either unjustly or unwisely in making us free to do good and also evil. To anyone asking: "Why then have we not been created impeccable?" Basil answers:

> Who reproaches the Creator for not having made man impeccable by nature does nothing other than to indicate a preference to be irrational rather than a rational creature, an immobile, inert being, deprived of the ability to be free and active.[3]

Basil, seeing well that human wisdom, a participation of God's own willing, can also be corrupted by error and sin, insists that our ability to be at least capable of constant change does not come from our human intellect and will, but rather "from being always in movement." Thus it is not our liberty or intellect which occasions our sinful fall, but it is our mutability, our fleeting character whereby the danger of a fall arises:

But there are in it [the human mind] two faculties; in accordance with the view of us who believe in God, the one evil, that of the demons which draws us on to their own apostasy; and the divine and the good which brings us to the likeness of God.[4]

Basil clearly saw that we freely choose evil rather than good. If we would remain fixed in contemplating the beauty and would persevere in the joy of the intelligible, we would have the ability and the power to lead a life conformed to its proper nature.[5] Unfortunately, however, we do not continue to live intelligently in keeping with our nature, made to God's image, and sin results. "Through a lack of vigilance it [our soul] grows heavy and falls from the superior regions. It mixes then with the flesh, goaded on by the desire of shameful joys of earthly pleasures."[6]

God alone is incorruptible and uncreated. We, through the gift of divine life, possess the childhood that can mature into an unending, eternal adulthood of participated divinity. Maturity for Irenaeus is to be gifted by the attributes of God as incorruptible and uncreated. But Adam lost this gift of life, and, though he possessed his human physical life, he became *corruptible* and *dead* as far as God's life within him was concerned. God cannot be at fault for Adam's disobedience and his fall from God's grace. Thus Irenaeus writes: "Those persons, therefore, who have apostatized from the light given by the Father and transgressed the law of liberty have done so through their own fault since they have been created free agents and possessed of power over themselves."[7]

St. Athanasius follows Irenaeus in insisting on human nature still remaining basically unchanged in its orientation to become "according to God's image." What is absolutely needed to return to divine life, Athanasius strongly preaches, is for God's only begotten Son to become enfleshed among us and thus restore us to true filiation by the divinization of the Holy Spirit. "The nature of man did not change. The difference is that man has clouded the light, hindered the plan of God and now the Son must come to replace man in the correct, logical path to beatitude and immortality."[8]

Sin in the Old Testament

As we have just seen from the representative writings of Irenaeus and Athanasius that typify the universal teachings of the patristic writers, the Eastern Fathers did not seek any philosophical definition of sin. They were solidly rooted in Holy Scripture. If King David could confess,: "I was born in guilt, a sinner from the moment of conception" (Ps. 51:5), so St. Paul could summarize the New Testament sense of sin in all human beings when he wrote, "As through one man sin entered into the world and through sin death.... Thus death has spread to all men because all have sinned" (Rom. 5:12).

Because we are tied to Adam's sin, all of us, according to Paul's teaching, find sin in our members (Rom. 7:24). There is that "unspiritual" self within all of us that Paul found dictating to him what he should do against God's law. He finds himself doing what he knows he should not do and not doing what he knows he should do (Rom. 7:14ff.). The sense of sin found in New Testament writings presupposes what is found in the Old Testament; both formed the double source of patristic teaching on the origin of human sin in the world.

In the Old Testament, there is no single word to denote sin. J. Pederson, in his work *Israel 1–11*, presents sin generally as a breach in God's loving and merciful covenant which he has made with his chosen people. The Hebrew words *het'* and *hatta't*, which are translated in the New Testament by the Greek word *harmatia,* mean "to miss the mark." This notion removes the merely legalistic view of sin based on deliberation to commit sin and broadens it to embrace the cause of sin as anything that prevents a human being, or the people of God, from living with God as the Center. It is failure to attain one's goal, one's end. Thus sin is unreality, insofar as it is considered "nonaction" in regard to the "real" action that brings fulfillment to the individual person or the community.

An important Hebrew word for sin in the Old Testament is *'awon*. It provides a context for understanding the richness of the concept of sin in the New Testament and therefore in the Eastern Fathers' teaching on sin. This word connotes a deviation, an element of failure and of distortion of something that should never have come into existence.

Sin in the New Testament can refer to sin as a single act, sin as a state or condition, or sin as a power. These latter two ideas are found often in the Pauline and Johannine writings. But the radical newness presented by the New Testament writers, and not found in the Old Testament, is that God has sent his own Son to conquer and destroy sin in the lives of those who believe in him as the Son of God. The magnitude of sin and the slavery that keeps the human race in absolute bondage through sin are highlighted only that we might accept the power of Jesus Christ as God's righteousness for us. God, through his Holy Spirit given us through Jesus' resurrection, redeems us and makes us righteous.

In the Old Testament we see that only God can deliver us from sin. In the New Testament the Good News is that God has done this through his Son, Jesus Christ. God, in his love, can do no more than he has already done for his people, his children, in giving them his Son as Deliverer and God's Righteousness.

Sin Brings Corruption

St. Athanasius has captured both the Old and New Testament concept of sin in showing the cosmic effects of Adam's refusal to live "according to God's image and likeness." We human beings without Christ's grace live in a cosmic condition that Athanasius calls *phthora,* which in Greek means "corruption." A process of disintegration takes place as a result of sin, which is described by Athanasius as a state wherein human beings lose the divine life of eschatological incorruptibility within themselves and become mortal, corruptible (i.e., deprived of divine life, or grace) and are "liable to the affections proper to nature."[9]

Adam's sin brought about this state of corruption (*phthora*). Into this state every human being is born, excluding Jesus Christ. Yet each human person is guilty for his or her own sins. Each person, yielding to self-idolatry (*philautia,* self-love), brings additional "corruption" into the world. Life according to the image and likeness of God is diminished, not only in the individual, but through him, in the subhuman cosmos, which now is no longer harmoniously moving back to God.

This seems to be the universal consensus of all the Eastern Fathers, who follow St. Athanasius in their commentaries on the well-known scriptural text Romans 5:12, as cited earlier.

St. Theodoret of Cyrus, the great leader of the Antiochene school and one of the architects of the Council of Chalcedon (451), interprets Romans 5:12 as Adam's sin bringing to all human beings "death." Today most New Testament scholars also follow his interpretation of the Greek phrase *eph'ho* as meaning the symbol of death as not only physical death, but also spiritual death to God's divine life in us: "Death, through which all have sinned, has passed to all men for it is not by the sin of the forefather that each man suffers the law of death, but from himself, from his own sins."[10]

Adam and Eve, having lost true incorruptibility, the divine life of God within them, could only beget children of "corruption" or mortality, death on all levels of existence, especially on the spiritual plane of total deprivation of God's life. Such mortal human beings are in such "mortality" committed to passions and fears and pleasures and sorrow.

Original Sin and Baptism

These insights from the early Fathers of the Eastern Churches could have great importance for Western Christians. In most theological manuals among Catholics and Protestants of the West, baptism is interpreted as a cleansing from original sin. If we study the ancient ritual of baptism, which today in the Eastern Churches is still received by infants along with Confirmation and the Eucharist, we find no stress placed on the removal of Adam's original sin. Rather we find through these ancient rituals the granting of divine life to the newly baptized. The new Christian is exhorted through the overshadowing power of the Holy Spirit to die with Christ to the "old creation" and put on the new creation in Christ Jesus (2 Cor. 5:17). The new Christian is liberated from this corrupt condition of death in which he or she was born and now a new life is freely bestowed for the Christian to live hidden in Christ Jesus.

As we become "immortal" in Christ by sharing in his divine life, we cease to be afraid of death, including our physical death. It is God's perfect love that casts out all fear (1 John 4:18). The sign of the new Christian is to be set free from the victory and sting of death (1 Cor. 15:55) It is precisely inasmuch as we become immortal in Christ that we cease to be afraid of death and can live in loving service to others, the true Christian test of already living in the immortal divine life of the Trinity through the risen Lord Jesus.

We can summarize, therefore, the Eastern Christian tradition of sin, especially the root of all our other personalized sins, original sin, as above all an inherited *mortality*. This leads the individual human being toward personal sins, but does not imply any guilt for the actual sin of Adam. This mortality, the consequence of Adam's sin and linked, more as cause than as effect, to the individual sins of his descendants, was transmitted by natural generation. Mortality and corruption were transmitted to every being except Jesus Christ. If Christ had come from a human sperm, he would not have been a new person. He was born into the human race, but not totally under the bondage of the effects of inherited "corruption" or mortality.

He could overcome death and restore human beings to true life and incorruptibility, which is divine life. For the Orthodox theologians the teaching of the Western Roman Church on the Immaculate Conception removes Mary, the Mother of God, from that which is inherited by every human being in birth. A greater understanding of the key issue of original sin perhaps can be of help to a better understanding of the relationship of human nature to grace.

To do this let us turn to the need to weep and mourn in order that we can truly experience what Jesus promised in the Beatitude: "Happy those who mourn: they shall be comforted" (Matt. 5:5).

CHAPTER SEVEN

Weep: There Is No Other Way!

ESTERN AS WELL AS EASTERN CHRISTIANS TODAY are seeking in the writings and traditions of the early Eastern Churches the elements of mysticism and direct experience with God that have always been a genuine element of all Christian prayer. Yet taking the classics of Christian mysticism literally or failing to transcend the cultural elements that form the backdrop of the times in which the ancient Eastern Christian writers lived can be a source of danger to modern Christian readers. Much in the writings of these early Fathers on the spiritual life must be demythologized to be meaningful to modern Christians.

91

When we are able to enter into their specialized linguistic symbols, expressions of a greater experience than any word-for-word translation can yield to us, perhaps then we will be able to see more clearly the substantial truths that are as applicable to our spiritual lives as they were to the lives of these early Christians.

Need for Compunction

One teaching stressed universally by all the early Eastern Fathers and Mothers of the desert that will always remain applicable for all Christians, regardless of time and place, when all the necessary demythologizing has been done, is their doctrine on *compunction*. They saw weeping for their sins as a necessary obligation for any Christian because this truth was integrally tied to the fundamental message of Christ's Gospel. "Blessed are they who mourn for they shall be comforted," was the exhortation of Christ and, therefore, also of Origen, Ephrem, Basil, Gregory Nazianzen, Gregory of Nyssa, John Chrysostom. In short, it is the common teaching of all the early Christian ascetics.

Typical of this patristic emphasis on weeping and mourning for one's sins and the sins of the world is the statement of Abbot Poemen of the fourth-century Egyptian desert Fathers:

> One of the brethren asked Abba Poemen, saying: "Father, what shall I do in the matter of my sins?" The old man said: "Whoever wishes to blot out his offenses can do so by means of weeping; for weeping is the path which the Scriptures have taught us, and the Fathers have also wept continually, and there is no other path except that of tears."[1]

The early monks fled into the deserts, where they reduced their needs to only the barest necessities for maintaining life. They purified themselves from all attachments in order to listen to God in the clear, pure air that is found only in deep silence and solitude.

In Holy Scripture they found the basis for what they considered a divine command: "To mourn according to God." The Old Testament uses the Greek word *penthos* 120 times to indicate the grief experienced by those in public or private mourning. Isaiah announced God's desire "to comfort all those who mourn and to give them for ashes a garland, for mourning robe the oil of gladness" (Isa. 61:3).

St. John Chrysostom in two works on compunction holds up David the psalmist as the model of those who practice *penthos*.[2] David's example encouraged the monks of old to imitate him: "I am worn out with groaning. Every night I drench my pillow and soak my bed with tears" (Ps. 6:6). David's *miserere* became a lesson in true Christian prayer: "Have mercy on me, O God, in your goodness; in your great tenderness wipe away my faults. Wash me clean of my guilt; purify me from my sin" (Ps. 51:1–2).

Chrysostom stresses that it is more important to experience compunction than to define it. Yet from the extensive patristic literature, consisting more in descriptive exhortations than in treatises defining compunction, we can gather some elements that constitute a working definition.

Thoughts that dwell on the individual's past infidelities toward a loving God effect a movement away from self-love to a passionate love of God. This leads to the existential awareness of man's own weakness and propensity toward evil, and hence to the consideration of the possibility of an eternity separated from God.

Other aids to foster an abiding sense of compunction recommended by the Fathers were frequent examination of conscience, especially in order to know oneself and one's weakness, and a constant state of vigilance before the attacks of the traditional eight thoughts that lead human beings into inordinate passions and a state of enslaving sin. Vigils, prayers, fasting, love of silence, the practice of human tasks and charitable works of service toward others all create an environment in which compunction can grow.

The Gift of Tears

Tears were considered a concrete criterion of a Christian's intense sorrow which, if it were real, gave a sense of identity to one's relationship to God. In this experienced unity tears flowed forth as a register of a sorrow that touched an individual at his or her deepest self. John Climacus writes in his seventh step: "Groanings and sorrows cry out to the Lord. Tears shed from awe and reverence intercede for us; but tears of all-holy love show us that our prayer has been accepted."[3]

Evagrius in his treatise on prayer (wrongly attributed to Nilus of Sinai) exhorts monks: "Before all else, pray to be given tears, that weeping may soften the savage hardness which is in your soul, and having acknowledged your sin unto the Lord (Ps. 31:5), you may receive from him the remission of sins."[4]

We tend today to fear sheer emotionalism, to say nothing of hysteria. A plethora of studies done on religious aberrations have made us cautious and suspect of anything not rooted in sound reason. As a result we may be losing a means that could greatly aid us in developing a more constant state of compunction. What the Fathers were seeking primarily in tears was a psychological state of persuasion that touched the individual Christian. It was not on any one level of sense or emotion or mind, but rather it was considered as a psychological state that touched one most deeply at the core of one's being. They distrusted any degree of interior compunction that did not also manifest itself in a reaction that flowed from their inner "core" outwardly into their senses. They surely had met neurotic persons who had wept tears in abundance, as Climacus states: "I have seen small tear drops shed with difficulty like drops of blood, and I have also seen fountains of tears poured out without difficulty. And I judged those toilers more by their toil than by their tears, and I think that God does too."[5]

They also knew tears could measure the interior compunction when the total person was deeply moved by sorrow. Climacus adds that "tears are the product of thought and the father of thought is a rational mind."[6] The Fathers applied to the spiritual life the same experience that is found in one's natural relationships to others, for if a person were to experience a great sorrow, regret, or fear of losing the most precious possession in life, that person would surely show this deeply felt emotion by tears.[7] Nilus of Sinai exhorted the deacon Agapet:

> Weep and pour forth tears before God by at least your desire and in this way you will be purified of your sins....In regard to this, I have known those who have not stopped there, but who by force of their faith and prayer have changed the rock of their soul into a source of water (Ps. 113:8). Thus spurring on their hearts without ceasing by the word of Christ and by the remembrance of the divine wonders, they have caused to burst forth from within outwardly a flood of tears flowing from eyes of stone.[8]

The desire to be penetrated with as deep a sorrow as possible before the goodness of God was stressed. The interior desire in itself was a spiritual weeping that the early Christians felt would turn to physical tears as a gift of God when the individual reached an intense and abiding sense of compunction. Compunction itself, deeply experienced, was the goal to be attained. The gift of tears was never desired as a separate "charism" in itself nor for the consolations the tears would bring the penitent.

Obstacles to a Sorrowing Heart

The Eastern Fathers were convinced that the reason religiously dedicated persons do not make continued progress in perfection is a lack of an abiding sense of sorrow. An examination of the obstacles to a living sense of compunction listed by the early Fathers might prove to be equivalent to an examination of our own personal failings in striving for perfection. In general, any neglect of spiritual exercises — such as frequent examination of conscience, serious meditation on the words and life of Christ along with his eschatological stress on one's end and judgment unto eternal reward or punishment — would cause a corresponding insensitivity in the human soul and open it to a spirit of dissipation.

The door would be open for the entrance of the eight passions that lead to inordinate attachments. *Parrhesia,* in the sense of an excessive looseness in uncontrolled speech, is one of the main avenues of dissipation and begets, in the words of St. Dorotheus, all other vices.[9] In fact, any excess or immoderation, which in itself indicates a self-centeredness and a failure to refer to God as our measure of proper conduct, must be avoided. This holds also in liturgical matters where overly elaborate chants and preoccupation with nonessentials can dry our hearts and take us away from the true occupation of adoring God through clearer knowledge of God and of oneself.

Overspeculation in a dry, rationalistic manner on theological problems constitutes another danger to compunction since it tends to make the theologian proud and creates a God too much according to one's own image. Especially destructive of the spirit of compunction for these desert athletes was excessive laughter. Here again, as in excessive and idle talk, boisterous laughter indicated a general lack of moderation and reflection. Clement, Origen, Ephrem, and John Chrysostom all insisted upon the impeding effects of immoderate laughter upon the gravity befitting a serious Christian who is in awe and reverence of God. St. Gregory Nazianzus permits "an affable smile or rather a trace of a smile, while holding in check by temperance any immoderation of laughter."[10]

Effects of Compunction

The greatest effect of compunction highlighted by the Fathers is the peace and joy that come through an experienced love of

God toward the sinful individual. This we can appreciate even if we have not all experienced it to the same degree as did those early great athletes of Christ. Purified of all inordinate, passionate desires, such monks knew a permanently abiding sense of tranquility that begot interior happiness. It was not the absence of troubles through a blind resignation to God's providence, as is often found in Islamic asceticism; nor was it a philosophical stoicism that basically feeds an inflated ego with a desire to be above all relationships to the world around it by simply ignoring the rest of the world.

This joy was at the basis of the Christian experience: *per crucem, ad lucem* (through the cross, to light). Compunction was the dying process and joy was the resurrection of all of one's powers into a new life that produced a hundredfold in peace and joy. Christ ended his beatitudes with the promise: "Rejoice and be glad, for a rich reward awaits you in heaven." Heaven was a condition that even in this life can be enjoyed to some ever-increasing degree by those who mourn for their sins.

The strangest paradox proved itself in experience as these early monks wept before God and God comforted them. Their interior joy, as their interior sorrow, had to manifest itself in the exterior countenance.

In a marvelous way experienced by all who seriously maintained themselves in this abiding compunction, God revealed himself to them, not in any conceptual knowledge deduced through a reasoning process, but in a direct, experiential knowledge that flooded the soul with an illumination of God's majestic grandeur. The shadows of dark sorrow mingle with the light of God's transcendence. And the Christian is content with repeating the only prayer that seems proper to the experience: "Lord, Jesus Christ, Son of God, have mercy on me, a sinner."

Paul Tillich, in a short essay entitled "The Eternal Now," shows how repentance is more than a feeling of sorrow about wrong actions. "It is the act of the whole person in which he separates himself from elements of his being, discarding them into the past as something that no longer has any power over the present."[11]

Compunction, for the early Fathers of the desert and for all Christians who have grasped their insights, is the means the Christian uses to live in the "eternal now," while living also in a past, present and future continuum. God, for the Fathers who wept "because there was no other way to perfection,"[12] was not a goal, an object toward which they moved and which they attained only upon death. God is the abundance of love that is ever overflowing in his uncreated energies that bombard his creatures at every moment. We are human beings, made to God's image and likeness and drawn to an intimate relationship of loving children of so loving a Father. In the past we have freely turned ourselves away from greater growth by sin. In the present and, hopefully by God's grace, in the future, we will feel the pull within and all around ourselves of a world that is "groaning in travail" (Rom. 8:22) until it reaches its perfection in Christ. This "existential angst" cries out for Another, One who lies beyond the ravages of time and space, One who is the possessor of all perfections, who makes all other possessions vain.

A Second Baptism

It is compunction, that abiding sorrow for the godless past and the fear of a future without God, that allows us to contact God in our brokenness. God gives himself to the weak, the poor, the needy, in a word, to the humble because they have entered into an experiential knowledge of their own creaturehood. The desert Fathers, crying incessantly with penitent David, "Thoroughly wash me, O Lord!" experienced a second baptism. Climacus writes: "But sins committed after baptism are washed away by tears."[13]

In this freedom from the past and the guilt that the future brings to us, we Christians of true compunction can gaze more clearly on the beauty and goodness of God. "Blessed are the pure of heart, for they shall see God" (Matt. 5:6). Filled with great tenderness and longing for greater union with God, Christians find their strength, not in their weakness, but in the merciful forgiveness of God. Because God has given them an abiding experience of their existential weakness, they are filled with great tranquility and joy since their strength is now in the all-powerful Father whom they experience mostly in God's tender forgiveness of their weaknesses.

Instead of becoming introverted, repentant Christians have a greater consciousness of their union with all nature, needing the cosmic redemption of God's condescending love. Charity and tenderness are extended to all, for who cannot now understand the need to love and aid the needy when we witness constantly the love and help of God shown already toward us?

Much is outdated and needs demythologizing in the writings of these fiercely serious Christians of an earlier age, but one truth will always remain the same, both for the monk in the desert of Egypt of the fourth century and for the Christian of the cybernetic society of the twenty-first century. We all have need of the baptism of Christ, received not once, but over and over renewed by our deeper conversion, whereby we are washed more and more of our own deep traces of resistance to God's love. We can receive the saving waters of baptism only if we cry out constantly. We are in continual need of God's recreating force in our lives. And yet God is always the forgiving Lover, ready to burst into our meaningless flow of consciousness in time with his meaningful presence that allows us to make of now the eternal *Now* of God.

CHAPTER EIGHT

Praxis: The Ascetical Life

IF TODAY many basically good Christians do not become outstanding, saintly persons, the reason perhaps may be the exaggerated misunderstanding coming down through the centuries that is attached to two long-established words in the Christian tradition of both East and West: "asceticism" and "mysticism." The teaching of the universal Church holds that both are inseparable elements in the development of a total Christian life.

Of the two terms, asceticism is perhaps the least acceptable for most modern Christians, since it projects an idea of religion that is a throwback to the self-sacrificing practices of the Middle Ages.

101

The basic reason why modern Christians have rejected the practice of asceticism is that it has come to mean an unhealthy withdrawal from this material world. Popular theology in the Middle Ages presented the "ascetical" sacrifices of Jesus Christ as an end to set us free and not as a means to divinize us mystically into loving children of the heavenly Father. Therefore ascetical practices became for the faithful only ends in themselves, something quite separate from the mystical life.

A Return to Asceticism

Despite the general aversion to asceticism and the ignorance about its true Christian meaning, there are hopeful signs of a change in the air. Many young people today, long pampered by their affluent society, have been turning to the Far Eastern religions and discovering there what self-discipline means and how to do it. Even older Christians are reacting negatively to the overindulgence of Western materialism that militates against any self-sacrifice. The ascetical practices that were observed in earlier times were swept away and nothing replaced them. Now many modern Christians see the need, above all, for inner self-discipline in order to live a good Christian life in a world careening crazily toward ever increasing self-indulgence.

Another reason for renewed interest in asceticism is a more biblical and theological anthropology, informed also by the behavioral sciences, that offers a holistic view of the human person as a total being with body, soul, and spirit relationships.[1] As our knowledge of God and ourselves as human beings changes through the insights from biblical theology and modern psychology, asceticism is seen as an important element in a positive development of a full human personality.

We have already studied the theological anthropology of the Eastern Fathers. The last chapter taught us the importance of being in touch with our inner brokenness and that of the entire world around us. Together we groan, weeping in our exiled alienation, for the Savior to heal the rift between ourselves and the Trinity.

Now we turn to the important teachings of the great mystical Eastern Fathers who, before they discoursed theologically on the great truths taught by Jesus Christ through his Church, lived literally in the deserts as ascetics. One of their great convictions is that *orthodoxia,* which in Greek means both "right praise of God" and also "right teaching," must be lived out in the lives of all Christians if such truths are to become "really real," by *orthopraxis,* which in Greek means "right living."

They did not systematize the Christian spiritual life as thoroughly and orderly as we find in Western spirituality. The Eastern Fathers never separated mysticism, the experiential life in the indwelling Trinity, from *praxis* (the ascetical life), that is, our own human activities and our cooperation with the trinitarian, uncreated energies of love.

The Eastern Fathers never lost sight of the interpersonalized relationships between the Trinity and ourselves. They did not separate their human nature as an independent area of human striving to "merit" grace and thus reach heaven. The spiritual life and its various stages of ongoing growth in union with the triune life are always seen in viewing God-Trinity as a community in loving, active relationships with all of creation.

The early Fathers viewed salvation as God's continued outpouring of self-sacrificing love for each person. For all are called to share the trinitarian life while on this earth. They called this human activity *praxis,* or the work of the human person to cooperate with God's grace in the restoring of "the image and likeness."

This activity on the part of the individual Christian consists fundamentally as a process of removing impediments that prevent us from living according to the divine Logos, Jesus Christ. This embraces the uprooting of all inordinate attachments in self-love (*philautia*) which then helps in the more positive development of a virtuous life modeled on that of Christ.

The Invisible Warfare

We see how universally all the Eastern Fathers, following the ascetical teachings of St. Paul, envisioned the spiritual life as an invisible battle with an invisible enemy. Our life on this earth is a struggle against the flesh, the princes, the powers, and the rulers of darkness, as Paul teaches in his letter to the Ephesians 6:12. Paul uses the term *ascesis,* which in Greek means to practice or to exercise. Paul exhorts the Corinthian Christians to practise vigilance and watchfulness with an intense effort similar to that put forth by athletes who must control their appetites if they are to win the crown as a prize for running in the race (1 Cor. 9:24).

The Eastern Fathers, therefore, consider asceticism to refer to any conscious self-control and systematic exercise of the Christian life in order to obtain the ultimate goal intended by God. They always saw such practices as a means, but a necessary means, to overcome all obstacles that prevent us from loving God with our whole heart and loving our neighbor as ourselves.

The first fundamental law of the "practical" part of the spiritual life envisions growth in perfection as a battle against the evil one who attacks us through our thoughts, called in Greek *logismoi.* In the patristic teaching regarding controlling the *logismoi,* our thoughts can be of both good and bad nature. Evagrius of Pontus, who lived in the Egyptian desert in the fourth century, taught that the *logismoi* are images, sensible phantasms, that, when dwelt upon, tend to draw us to that object existing outside of ourselves. It is dealing with a reality that is not evil in itself, but, given our fallen nature and the distension introduced through the effects of original sin, we are easily drawn to those things. These are a part of Paul's "unspiritual self" that wars within him, seeking to destroy him but enticing him to do the opposite of what his better self tells him is God's holy will (Rom. 7:22–24).

Symeon the New Theologian expressed well the teaching of Evagrius and the other earlier desert Fathers in regard to temptations and the absolute necessity on the part of any human being to enter into warfare against such inimical forces:

> Warfare goes on constantly, and the soldiers of Christ must at all times be armed with their weapons. Neither by night nor by day nor for a single instant is this warfare interrupted, but even when we eat or drink or do anything (1 Cor. 10:31) we find ourselves in the thick of battle. On all human beings there lies the inescapable necessity of joining in this conflict. No one may escape the alternatives of either winning and staying alive or of being overcome and dying.[2]

The Eastern ascetics have followed St. John Climacus's teaching on the development of thoughts within us. Climacus refers to five steps in the presentation of the *suggestion,* and the ensuing dialogue in our mind that determines how we respond to such temptations. The mere suggestion is never sinful in itself, but can be an energy event brought about, as Isaac the Syrian points out, from natural desires of the flesh, from our imagination, from stored-up sense phantasms, from anticipated opinions as we allow them to be called forth by our mind, and lastly from the insults of the devils waging war against us and leading us to vice.[3]

We either live out our baptismal vow to deny Satan and his wiles and choose to live according to the virtues of Jesus Christ or we surrender to the temptation and choose to remain a slave to carnal-mindedness. The second stage is the coupling or conversation with the image (in Greek: *sunduasmos*). This is a dialogue with the suggestion presented that leads then to the possibility of the third step: the giving of consent to the thought. What follows this stage is the slavery or captivity where we are caught by the evil one.

The final stage is what the Fathers call *pathos,* or passion. This does not refer to the powerful concupiscible and irascible passions found in all human beings as a vital part of the goodness of one's human nature. The word "passion," in the context of *pathos,* refers to our own free activity in yielding to evil thoughts and our creating by such choices within us a habit that holds us in its evil enthrallment.[4]

Vices and Virtues

Evagrius of Pontus first developed the psychology of the eight principal vices from which flow most temptations. He writes:

> There are eight principal thoughts, from which all other thoughts stem. The first thought is of gluttony; the second, of fornication; the third, of love of money; the fourth of discontent [*acedia*]; the fifth, of anger; the sixth, of despondency; the seventh, of vainglory; the eighth, of pride. Whether these thoughts disturb the soul or not does not depend on us; but whether they linger in us or not and set passions in motion or not, does depend on us.[5]

The Latin ascetical writers hold seven capital sins, beginning with pride as the first and root of all other sins. Evagrius begins his list of eight capital passions, or vices, with gluttony, which is more empirical since a temptation usually moves from some sensible good toward a more intellectual one.

The more positive element of *praxis* as lived by the Eastern Fathers is the development of virtues by putting on "the mind of Christ" (Eph. 4:17), by an inner revolution. St. Maximus the Confessor makes clear the connection of virtues and our relationship with Christ: "For the substance of all the virtues is our Lord Jesus Christ himself.... All human beings, therefore, who, by constant fidelity acquire such virtue, participate without doubt in God — the substance of all the virtues."[6]

One basic conviction among all the Eastern ascetics was that all virtues are interrelated and all are acquired during the struggle to overcome any given temptation. Pseudo-Macarius writes:

All the virtues are mutually bound to each other. Like a certain spiritual chain, one is dependent upon the other; prayer to love, love to joy, joy to meekness, meekness to humility, humility to service; service to hope, hope to faith, faith to obedience, obedience to simplicity.[7]

Love above All

The Fathers place great stress on inner attention, or the guarding of the heart (in Greek, *prosochi*) This refers to the necessary inner discipline to be attentive in the very suggestion of a thought and whether the thought will lead to good and greater union with Christ or to greater self-centeredness.

One of the favorite words used in Greek to describe such an inner alertness is *nepsis. Nepo* means to be sober, not to be inebriated or intoxicated. It is a mental "sobriety," a mental balance in the presence of the indwelling Spirit to discern what would give God the greater glory in regard to our accepting or rejecting a given suggestion. Thus *nepsis* is not only the interior awareness of the possibility of evil forces coming in by way of infiltrating thoughts; it is also the whole development through vigilance of the virtuous correspondence to God's voice within us.

We could call this the reintegration of the human being, a returning as a total person to one's true self in Christ Jesus as God had originally created each of us. Such a struggle will never cease in this life, for there will always exist the danger of falling through accepting the temptations that would lead us to sin. It is through *nepsis* that we attain such a control over our senses and all our interior faculties so that we can hear and accept lovingly to choose always in the Word of God. Thus we find within ourselves a unity, a harmony, that is achieved only through great fidelity to the interior living Word.

Apatheia is the word that Evagrius and his successors use to describe the state or process of becoming progressively more "dispassionate," i.e., not under the slavery of carnal-mindedness, and of being at all times docile to the movements of the Holy Spirit. This is far from any Stoic "apathy." It does not consist in the extirpation of the God-given passions and emotions; rather it is in the proper control of these passions that we find our growth in Christian sanctity. The great aim of the Eastern Fathers is to achieve through virtue and through the self-control of our natural passions the complete surrendering of ourselves in every thought and desire to do the holy will of God. John Climacus summarizes the essence of *apatheia*:

> By dispassion [*apatheia*] I mean no other than the interior heaven of the mind, which regards the tricks of the demons as mere toys. And so he is truly dispassionate, and is recognized as such who has made his flesh incorruptible, who has raised his mind above creatures and has subdued all his senses to it, and who keeps his soul in the presence of the Lord, ever reaching out to him even beyond his strength. Some say that dispassion is the resurrection of the soul before the body; but others, that it is the perfect knowledge of God, second only to that of the angels.... The soul has dispassion which is immersed in the virtues as the passionate are in the pleasures.[8]

Ascetical perfection is not measured by the difficulty of the practices performed, but rather by how unswervingly a person directs everything toward God. Authentic Christian sanctity according to the Eastern Fathers consists in flexibility to move in every event, in every thought, word, and deed, toward God. Asceticism reflects such a faith that embraces the cross of self-denial, that becomes a positive obedience to the heavenly Father through Jesus Christ and the Holy Spirit.

Thus an asceticism of the cross as taught by Jesus and the desert Fathers is ultimately an asceticism of love that moves the individual irrevocably away from self-centeredness to a God-centering. It is a singleness of vision that makes God the only criterion of our choices: "If your eye is sound, your whole body will be filled with light" (Matt. 6:22). It is the seed falling into the ground and dying in order to bring forth much fruit (John 12:24).

As we experience in prayer and in our daily life the abundant love of God, we are moved to want to go beyond the negativity and positivity involved in fulfilling at all times the commands and the wishes of the Father. This Jesus shows us as he sought to please always his Father (John 8:29). This is where human freedom reaches its peak and asceticism moves into mysticism.

Purity of Heart

St. John Cassian, who brought Eastern asceticism and mysticism to Western monasticism, shows the unanimous teaching of the Fathers, who saw asceticism and mysticism linked through what they consistently called "purity of heart." He writes:

> The goal of our profession is the kingdom of God. Its immediate purpose, however, is purity of heart, for without this we cannot reach our goal. . . . We do everything for the sake of this immediate purpose. All these things [of the ascetical life] establish purity of heart; and it is for this that we should do everything. It is useless, therefore, to boast of our fasting, vigils, poverty and reading of Scripture when we have not achieved the love of God and our fellow human beings.[9]

Thus we see why the Eastern Fathers did not conceive the spiritual life as a movement from one stage of purgation to that of illumination in Christ, finally to arrive at the unitive way with God. Rather they saw three interrelated relationships as they worked together to bring the Christian into true wisdom, *gnosis,* experiential knowledge of all things in Christ, God's Logos, in whom all things have their being. This *gnosis* leads to true love, *agape. Praxis* touches the area of our activity to discipline us in order to lead us to the first stages of infused contemplation, which

Maximus the Confessor calls *theoria physica*. After purification we should move to a contemplation of the exterior world. This world brings us to the inner world beyond the sensible, the phenomena. It is here that we encounter the mind of God through the infusion of deeper faith, hope, and love of the Holy Spirit to see the *logoi* in all of God's creatures, as was pointed out in chapter 4.

The third stage of the spiritual life according to Evagrius and Maximus constitutes what the Eastern Fathers called "true theology." The term is not used in our Western sense of speculative theology, divorced from the experience of the *mystical*. It rather refers to the mystical contemplation of the Holy Trinity, indwelling within us and also in all of God's creatures as *uncreated energies of love*.

In the highest type of contemplation the Christian progresses farther and farther from earthly thoughts to become gradually assimilated to God. The principle that guides all theory of contemplation and divinization in the Christian East is that like can be known only by like. True knowledge of the Trinity can be given to us only in the proportion that we are assimilated to the likeness of God through the "two hands": Jesus Christ and the Holy Spirit, to quote St. Irenaeus.[10]

It is through *praxis* that the obstacles to a more intimate knowledge of God are removed. It is through *theoria physica* that the mind of God is discovered in his effects upon the created world through his Logos. It is through *theoria theologica,* God speaking about himself, that a direct knowledge of God as Trinity is given to the individual.

Without charity, *praxis* and *apatheia* would become mere stoicism. Without charity contemplation would become mere philosophical speculation. For Maximus the Confessor charity proceeds in steps. The first is charity as the virtue that insures the presence of all other virtues in the attainment of harmony within us. This then feeds contemplation, through which we discover the mind of God in all things so we can live always in God's Logos made flesh, Jesus Christ. The final goal of all of us is the charity toward the Trinity, and this admits of an unending growth in this life and in the life to come. For Maximus charity is like an embryo that grows through our continued, active cooperation with the uncreated energies of the Trinity.[11]

Paul summarizes the goal of all our activities that make up our spiritual life and without which we are not truly "spiritualized" by the Holy Spirit, who is the gift of love: "In short, there are three things that last: faith, hope, and love; and the greatest of these is love" (1 Cor. 13:13).

CHAPTER NINE

Jesus Christ: The Savior of the World

E HAVE ALREADY SEEN in the previous chapters the necessary elements that constitute the theological and anthropological views of the Eastern Fathers. These were the basis for their development of an *orthodox* teaching of the most elemental truth, the keystone on which the Christian faith is constructed, namely, a right teaching concerning Jesus Christ as true God and yet true man and how he is the Redeemer and Savior of God's entire created order. Now we turn to the writings of the early Eastern Fathers to see how they developed their traditional teaching of Jesus Christ as the sole Redeemer and Savior through whom all of creation will be restored and will reach fulfillment in and through Jesus Christ and the Holy Spirit.

Recapitulation

The Greek Orthodox theologian Constantine N. Tsirpanlis approaches the traditional views of Eastern Christian theologians on the understanding of the meaning of redemption or salvation:

> The conception of *soteria* in the Eastern Church and the patristic tradition is broader and more inclusive than the Roman Catholic emphasis on "redemption" and "reconciliation" and the Protestant "justification." The Orthodox Church prefers to use the term *soteria* also because the New Testament uses that term (about forty times) in order to describe the work accomplished by Jesus Christ (and the title given to Christ: *soter* about twenty times).[1]

Irenaeus was the first Christian theologian to formulate a restored anthropology in and through Jesus Christ. He was the first to describe the purpose of the incarnation of God's Word into the human race. Christ shows forth to us human beings the perfect image of God (Col. 1:15). He comes to restore the similitude or likeness of God to us. In a theological synthesis amazing for its time, the double mysticism of St. John and St. Paul coalesce. Irenaeus mingles the two elements: the identification of the flesh of Christ with ours and the promise of eternal life because Christ is the Prince of Life who ontologically lives within us through God's uncreated grace. He writes:

> The Word of God was made a son of man in order that we may receive the adoption and become a child of God.... How could we have been able to be united to incorruptibility and immortality if *Incorruptibility* and *Immortality* did not first become that which we are?[2]

To describe the role of Christ as the Second Adam, the restorer of a cosmos grown sick with self-love, Irenaeus uses the Pauline word *anakephalaiosis,* meaning "recapitulation."[3] Many commentators of Irenaeus have labored to define his precise use of this word, for he uses it as a framework within which he constructs the first articulated Christian theology of redemption as well as a Christian anthropology.[4]

His theory of recapitulation structures his theological system. It signifies a rebeginning of the human race, whereby Christ reverses the process that had turned earth away from true Light, Life, and Incorruption toward sin, chaos, and death. God gathers up in his Logos his entire work by fulfilling it according to his original plan through an intimate association with the living Logos in the individual human being, made according to the image and likeness of God which is Christ. The "logosized" creature, in union with the other creatures of the universe, is restored in Christ to reach the *pleroma* (the fullness or completion) in Christ's glorious second coming, his *parousia.*

The term, therefore, can mean a resumé, a taking up of all since the beginning, a recommencement, a return to the source, a restoration, a reorganization and incorporation under one head. Included in this comprehensive, imaginative concept is the idea that Christ the Redeemer underwent all the trials of Adam, but with total success. Christ does not merely undo, detail by detail, all that Adam had done to bring the human race into its fallen state. Basing his theology of Christ's restoration of the human race on a dynamic concept of growth and conflict, Irenaeus presents Christ as the champion of the human race, who also enters into the fray to do battle with the Evil One.

Yet Christ the Victor does not merely restore creation to what it was in the beginning. He completes it through a process of growth as a human person grows from embryo, through childhood, to full manhood.

The term *anakephalaiosis* (recapitulation) springs initially from Ephesians 1:10: God decreed "to gather [*anakephalaiosasthai*])

all creation both in heaven and on earth under one head, Christ."
But Irenaeus advances the content of the term:

> Christ has therefore in his work of recapitulation summed
> up all things, both waging war against our enemy and crush-
> ing him who at the beginning had led us away captive in
> Adam...in order that, as our species went down to death
> through a vanquished man, so we may ascend to life through
> a victorious one.[5]

Not Assumed, Not Saved

Origen, Athanasius, the Cappadocian Fathers, Basil, Gregory of
Nazianzus and Gregory of Nyssa, and Cyril of Alexandria all
build their theology of Christ as Redeemer and Savior upon the
writings of Irenaeus. Christ's birth and maturing is the first creation among human beings brought to perfection. Christ is the
human person in his fullest completion, as God had originally
planned all of us to be "in Christ." In the incarnation a single
human being came into existence, but he contained and developed to the fullest all the purity and life that the entire world had
lost. Christ is fully all that we ought to be. There is in him nothing of sin, of aversion from God through Adam's sin. In Christ's
humanity, God lays hands on us again. Those hands, the divine
Logos and the Holy Spirit, will effect a "new creation" through
the humanity of Christ, making all human beings one with him.

St. Athanasius, in his valiant fight against the heresy of Arianism that denied that Jesus was truly God, the divine Logos, from
all eternity, developed the insights of Irenaeus. He simply asked
the question: "What was God to do?" His answer was that God
could only recreate the lost relationship to the divine image and
destroy corruptible death:

> What was to be done except the renewing of that which was
> in God's image, so that by it human beings might once more

be able to know him? But how could this come to pass save
by the presence of the very image of God, our Lord Jesus
Christ? Whence the Word of God came in his own person,
that, as he was the image of the Father, he might be able
to create afresh human beings after the image. But, again, it
could not else have taken place had not death and corruption
been done away....None other then was sufficient for this
need, save the image of the Father.[6]

St. Gregory Nazianzus gives us his basic principle used against
Apollonarius, who held that Christ had a defective human nature,
not possessing the full human reasoning powers. This principle,
which the subsequent Eastern Fathers would repeat constantly, is:
"What is not assumed by Christ is not saved; that alone is saved
which is united with God."[7] Precisely because the divine Logos
was a perfect human being, it was made possible through his humanity for the divine Logos to make contact with other human
beings and thus bring redemption to individuals.

Gregory's writings, especially his sermons and poems, are char-
acterized by vigorous, forceful language to express the reality of
the incorporation of the individual through a most personal, intimate union with Christ. The events of Christ's life on this earth,
his activities and his miracles, are being renewed in our souls. The
passion of Christ is taking place today. He is suffering today in the
sense that his members are suffering with him. He sustains them
by his indwelling divine life.

Yesterday I was crucified with him; today I am glorified with
him; yesterday I was buried with him; today I am quickened
with him; yesterday I was buried with him; today I rise with
him.... Let us offer ourselves, the possession most precious
to God, and most fitting; let us give back to the Image what
is made after the Image. Let us recognize our dignity; let us
honor our Archetype; let us know the power of the mystery
and for what Christ died. Let us become like Christ, since

Christ became like us. Let us become God's for his sake since he for us became man.[8]

The redeeming work of Christ in the world according to Gregory of Nazianzus begins in the depths of each person, in Christ's transformation of the individual person into a child of God. Thus the incarnation and redemption of Christ are dynamically viewed, not simply as historical events in past time and space, but as Christ's activities going on in an event here and now in the interior life of the individual person as he renews the face of the earth. An *I-Thou* relation with Christ is established through his living presence within the individual soul. To live with Christ is to act as a new creature with him.

> I must be buried with Christ, arise with Christ, be joint heir with Christ, become the child of God, yea, God himself.... This is the purpose for us of God, who for us was made man and became poor to raise our flesh and recover his image and remodel us that we might all be made one in Christ who was perfectly made in all of us all that he himself is...that we may bear in ourselves only the stamp of God, by whom and for whom we were made and have so far received our form and model from him that we are recognized by it alone.[9]

Participating in the Second Adam, Christ, we are divinized already in part and fully only after death, when we will achieve union with him in heaven. We must enter, therefore, into Christ in this life by putting on the vision of life that Christ in his humanity possessed. We must see this material world, above all, the reality of suffering, with now a partial and eventually a full resurrection, from Christ's view.

By relating his fundamental soteriological principle, namely, "nothing is redeemed unless Christ has assumed it," not only to our human composition of body and soul, but to all facets of human existence and activity, Gregory opened the way again for an incarnational presence of Christ within the entire cosmic world, though he did not produce a systematic theology of Christ's cosmic presence.

Christ the Perfect Adam

Gregory of Nyssa saw the reality of God's creation as primarily present in his transcendent eternal decree. We might call it a fourth-dimensional view that allows him to see the beginning (not chronologically, but in the order of God's finality) as coterminous with the end, the *eschaton*. Measured history, therefore, is a dynamic process, a fulfillment of the divine unified idea of the cosmos, wherein the end coincides with the beginning. God's idea of the created world in and through the Logos, which he possesses from all eternity, will be realized in the *pleroma* exactly as he has conceived it, outside of time. Thus one of the great hurdles of Western theological thinking is cleared, namely, the union of nature and supernature. We human beings are viewed *in toto* and never are seen outside of God's redemptive plan in and through Jesus Christ.

Gregory, influenced by Origen, saw in the Genesis account of the creation of the first human being, Adam, the ontological "every human person." The first man, Adam, stands for the universal human being, every human person, who has been made by God to his image and likeness. Thus the first human being and the final, perfected human being are alike.[10] Gregory, in his work *The Creation of Man,* insists that before Adam, historically the first man, human's nature in the mind of God was already perfect and realized in and through Jesus Christ.[11]

Yet we human beings alone could not respond positively to God's ideal plan. A greater, more perfect being, one who already had attained the state to which we were all aspiring, was needed; one who could inspire not only by his example, but also by his activity, could effect in us this "return." This more perfect being had to be none other than the very Lord of our human nature, for he had given to us our existence, and only he could restore us to participation in his own divine likeness.[12]

Redemption is described by Gregory mainly in terms of restoration by Christ of the image according to which we all have been created. Christ was "transfused by our nature in order that our nature might by this transfusion of the Divine become itself divine."[13] Being united to a divine person, Christ's humanity was perfectly divinized. Hence his human nature "returned" to the state before the fall. Christ's humanity, through his human oblation of self to God, became deified. He was the perfect human being according to which model God conceived our full human nature. We, by our human nature as conceived in the *eternal now* of God's decree, signifies, of necessity, a relationship to Christ. It is necessary if we are to be perfectly fulfilled.

Christ's humanity still lives inserted into our universe, drawing us to the "return" or fulfillment in accordance with his own image. His redeeming, restorative activity extends to all human beings.[14] It is through Christ's resurrectional activities in us that he can touch and change the universe into glory to the Father. Christ is the Living Word in us, suggesting our good thoughts and working in us to do good deeds. Individuals begin by contemplating the divine activity of Christ within themselves. This activity of the prolonged incarnation in our lives extends to the universe.

Maximus the Confessor

Yet Gregory of Nyssa was rarely concerned with the rest of material creation. In God's providence this would be the task of St. Maximus the Confessor (d. 662). Although he is best known as the one who synthesized the orthodox teaching on Christ as Redeemer and Savior as defined in the Council of Chalcedon (451), Maximus interests modern readers more because of the cosmic dimensions of his synthesis of the whole created order, a harmonious union with God in and through Christ.

He renews and develops the central idea found in the writings of St. Irenaeus on the recapitulation of the whole universe in Christ. He sees the whole world in the light of the incarnation. Polycarp Sherwood, a patristic authority on the theology of Maximus, finds this to be the key to Maximus's speculation that has influenced all later Eastern Fathers, especially Gregory Palamas:

> For the coherence of Maximus' thought...does not derive from the systemization of the Church's teaching in function of some humanly posited principle or philosophy, but from a vision of divine things in the light of the Incarnation of the Son of God, in the light therefore of that mystery by which alone we know the Father and our salvation.[15]

Maximus saw more clearly than his predecessors that only a proper understanding of the purpose of the incarnation of Christ and his resurrection would yield a true understanding of the cosmos as it was created and destined by God. From this mystery he derived his fundamental law that would provide the keystone to his synthesis of the universe.[16]

Both as the preexistent divine Logos and as fullness of existing human nature, Jesus Christ is the bond providing the unity of intelligibility and of cosmic energy (love) that are hidden beneath the surface of the material appearances of creatures. The *logos* of each creature is its principle of harmony that shows us the relationship of a given creature to God's total providence and to the total order of salvation. The whole world is interlocked and interrelated, but only thinking human beings are capable of seeing the harmonious relationship between the *logoi* and the Logos.[17]

Maximus conceives the Logos on different levels of incarnational activity. He first sees him as the preexistent second person of the Trinity, the Word that speaks eternally the Mind of the Father and hence is the model according to which all creatures have their fullness. Next Maximus understands the Logos more precisely as a parallel to the historical incarnation. The Logos, God-man, gloriously resurrected, is inserted into the material world and is actively working to bring both human beings and the subhuman cosmos to the likeness of the divine ideas possessed by the preexistent Logos.

The harmony and unity between the *logoi* and Logos is effected by us who by contemplation learn to see the intelligibility "within" the created order and learn in love to live according to God's purpose. But to see the *logoi* in all creatures, we must submit to the illuminating activity of the Logos. Maximus writes in his *Four Centuries on Charity*:

> Just as the sun when it rises and lights up the world manifests both itself and the things lit up by it, so the Sun of Justice, rising upon a pure mind, manifests itself and the essences of all things that have been and will be brought to pass by it.[18]

Only he who has this gift from the Logos to see beyond the appearances can unlock the world and see the harmony existing among all creatures. He is able to enter partially into God's very purpose, into God's very mind, to see the raison d'être of each created being.

The Church

Christ's transforming activities through the power of the Holy Spirit continue in the cosmos through the Church. In the Church the living Logos is preached, and through the sacraments Christ is encountered in his resurrectional life by the Christian faithful. As has been pointed out, the supreme work of God living in us is to effect a unity among disjointed creatures, separated from their Creator and from one another by ignorance and sin. It is the work of the Church to achieve this unity and it does this first by unity of faith in the teachings of revelation.

If we are to be sanctified and approach to the likeness of God in and through Jesus Christ and the Holy Spirit in holiness, hence be united with the Trinity in thought and affection, it must be through an exact profession of the faith. Subjectivism and self-delusion are overcome by obedient submission to the teaching hierarchy that Christ established over his Church.[19] It is the Church that exposes to us the incarnate Christ, living in his glorious resurrected life to be encountered by us through the sacraments. Baptism administered by the Church opens to us the fruits of the incarnation. It is especially in the reception of the divine Logos and High Priest in the Holy Eucharist that we are divinized and are able to fulfill Christ's priestly function of making all things holy.

We conform ourselves to the Logos present by grace within us. Then we are able, through the enlightenment of the Logos, to perceive the *logoi* in other creatures and to perform the role of priest by offering a sacrifice of praise and glory to God through our proper use of creatures. Christ sacrifices himself totally in the Eucharist to give himself to us in order that we, through the use of our illumined reason, might be raised to the perfection of Christ.[20]

The Church itself is the unifier of all that divides us from one another. It achieves an ecclesial unity which is not only a type of the future cosmic unity, but is the basis for it. It is the human race already united in the fullness of Christ, but not yet fully in all the cosmos.[21] We human beings stand at the center of the cosmos. Deified human beings, in whom God lives and through whom he acts to fulfill the world, are the mediators between the disparate and disjointed world and the unity that has been achieved perfectly in the God-man's humanity through the incarnation.

Maximus insists over and over on the intimate connection between our deification and the transfiguration of the material cosmos. We, permeated by grace, achieve a unity within ourselves which allows us to effect a cosmic unity in the material world around us as we live and act according to the divine Logos made flesh. We can quote again the words of Vladimir Lossky to summarize Maximus the Confessor's Christology and ecclesiology that represent the fullness of Orthodox theology: "In his way to union with God the human person in no way leaves creatures aside, but gathers together in love the whole cosmos disordered by sin, that it may at last be transfigured by grace."[22]

New Creation

It is this total, unified vision of the early Eastern Fathers that is most enriching for us in the modern world. By viewing our relations to God, to other human beings, and to the rest of the created world from the fourth dimension of God's finality, they were able to avoid the dichotomy that in the West was mainly responsible in theological thought for the diminishment of the cosmic dimension of Christ's activity in our present world.

Rather than an antithesis between *nature* and *supernature,* they opposed *natural* and *unnatural*. *Nature* was not only the embryonic seed, but the fulfillment in all the creatures' final fruition. Our nature was always destined, not only by God's finality in creating us, but also in God's loving activity to accomplish his plan, to make us divinized children of God. Our total entity, body, soul, and spirit (with God's divine life dwelling in us and guiding us in all our choices according to his divine Spirit) was to move in a continuous process of loving activities in the cosmos to a more conscious, loving relationship to the divine Trinity.

In following the giant footsteps of Paul and John, the Eastern Fathers had secured the transcendence of God the Creator and the centrality of us human beings in the created world as the cocreators with the Trinity by stressing that we possessed in our intellect and will the seeds of a likeness to God in grace. They stressed that Jesus Christ was not only the perfect model, the Image of the Father according to whom we and the whole cosmos were created, but that through his incarnation he was also in the midst of the material world exerting his power to bring the whole created order into its fullness through the instrumentality of other human beings, motivated by reciprocal love towards Christ.

The Church is the sign wherein the created cosmos enters into a transfiguration, and through its instrumentality the resurrectional life of Jesus Christ is extended to the cosmos. Retaining its own individuality, each creature is able to be assumed into a new transcendent relation with God as its end. The material world, through the Church, meets the Spirit. Retaining its materiality, it still participates in a new spirituality. The *eschaton,* through the Church, has been realized in the *now,* but *not yet* fully. The resurrection of Christ is applied to the transformation of the world into "God in all" to the degree that the baptized in Christ rise from a self-centered life to put on a new life in him. The rest of the world waits for us to stretch out in yearning (*ecstasis*) that will be climaxed only in the *parousia* when Jesus Christ shall come to render explicit what was always implicit, to reveal what was hidden, to fructify the powers in creation which were lying there in potency. He will accomplish this with our free-will cooperation to be coreconcilers of all creation as we live in him in the *New Creation* (2 Cor. 5:17–18).

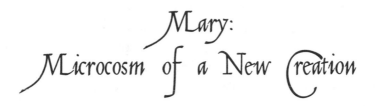

CHAPTER TEN

Mary:
Microcosm of a New Creation

N THE FOURTH CENTURY the rusty hinges that held together the tired, weary Roman Empire of the Caesars fell clanging to the ground. A new dynamic force swept through the land. Christianity, like a silent leaven, was raising humanity to a new level of community. The Church of Jesus Christ, his Body, was being formed again by those broken and contrite of heart. The little ones were being chosen to preach God's immense love for humankind. The weak ones of this earth were confounding the mighty. Although Constantine saw the sign of the conquering cross in the heavens, the triumph would come first in the hearts

127

of the meek and humble, who lovingly embraced the crosses that always come with living in love for others in humble service.

I believe we are beginning a new age. The sign in the heavens replacing the age of Aquarius is Virgo-Mater. The Virgin-Mother is the *Woman* entering into the pangs of childbirth. She is Mary-Church, a community of love through self-sacrificing emptiness that allows a diversity and unity in a paradox of harmony through love. Evil forces seek to swallow up her child as it is being born, but she will succeed and bring it to birth with a great progeny of other children.

The Orthodox faithful of the East kept the ancient devotion to Mary as virgin and mother and, therefore, the archetype of the feminine contemplative spirit that lies as the integrating, healing force between our human consciousness and our unconscious. In the symbol of Mary as virgin we see ourselves as individuals and as Church, the community of individuals brought into unity by the Spirit of the risen Jesus.

Virginity on this primeval level is each human being opening to God's initial love in total surrendering obedience. It is the letting go of our lives in faith and childlike trust in God to let him have full centrality in our lives.

Analogy and Archetype

The analogy of Mary and the Church has been in the Church from earliest times. The perspective of the early Church Fathers has always been one of Mary and the Church essentially in the christological order of the economy of salvation. The primary interest of the Fathers in linking Mary, an individual, the first Christian, with the whole of the Body of Christ, the Church, and vice versa, was always to highlight the plan of salvation, seen from the designs of God.

They viewed the redemption of the human race as an action descending from God through space and time. This process reaches its most decisive realization when the Blessed Virgin Mary conceived the divine Word. But there is a continuity in the process, according to the plan of God, so that the Church carries on, fulfills, realizes the same mystery that Mary so perfectly fulfilled in microcosmic dimensions in effecting the hypostatic union.

Mary and the Church are in an analogous way the same thing, but two different moments in the action of God descending to humankind and the material cosmos, which have already been redeemed in the archetypal, microcosmic form of Mary and to some extent of the Church.

The more we can recapture the patristic viewpoint, the more we will replace Mary at the head of the receiving humanity and the more we will see Christ as the active agent sent from the Father in order to draw us back to him through the instrumentality of the Church. This patristic view will also constitute the best rapprochement among the Orthodox, Catholics, and Protestants.

By considering the Church more as the Mystical Body of Christ, as the Spouse of Christ and the Mother of the people of God, the more we will present a Church that is more biblical and more in keeping with the early traditions of the Church. But to do this we must go to the Fathers and see how they viewed Mary as the archetype, the microcosm, of the Church and in God's plan of the entire macrocosm of his created world.

"Archetype" is derived from two Greek words, *arche* and *tupos,* both of which have double referents. In its primary meaning *tupos* refers to a physical blow and to the concrete manifestation of its impact, e.g., a seal and its imprint or the cast that molds the statue and the statue itself. Both are types.[1]

In biblical literature the derived meanings are found, e.g., when St. Paul compares in the ontological and moral order Adam as the type of the future New Adam, Christ. Essentially the scriptural meaning, especially in the New Testament writings, can mean a personification or representation of a spiritual unity through some sort of image. It can also imply the real bond existing between one entity and another as the objective foundation of this relationship. The third meaning can be a moral example as a result of this relationship.

The first element of an archetype is found in mariology in the person of Mary as a spiritual entity in tangible form that contains or represents what would unfold in future Christians, in the ontological purpose and essence of the Church as a whole, and eventually in the recapitulation of the entire material world through the cosmic Christ.

The second meaning of archetype brings us to the essential element that provides us with Mary's ontological relationship to the Church. Between Mary and the Church there is a consequent real, inner connection linking the two together. In this sense Mary is a type of Church, representing its innermost essential nature and her personal figuration brings the Church closer to us.[2]

Mary: The New Eve

The basic points of similarity between the archetype, Mary, and the type, Church, the individual Christians and ultimately in God's designs the entire material cosmos center around the virginity and motherhood of the Church and of Mary. The Church gives birth to the members of Christ's Mystical Body through the sacraments and through the faith handed down through the apostolic teachings. It is a virgin through its unblemished faith, its tenacity to orthodoxy, its espousal to Christ through divine grace. We find the grounds for this predication in the biblical language of Christ as the New Adam and the Church as the New Eve.

Mary has the same two qualities, but realized in a different manner. She is corporeally the mother of Christ and physiologically is a virgin. Yet spiritually, too, in the designs of God, she plays the role of the New Eve in restoring the human race to the pristine life of God through sanctifying grace.

In a language that shows a relaxed typological thought, the Eastern Fathers could move, not only back and forth, speaking of both the Church and Mary at the same time, but could even apply a similar type of virginity and maternity to the individual Christian in whom God is born through grace and through a virginal espousal to Christ, where the "two will become as one flesh."

The earliest Greek Fathers, Justin and Irenaeus, and the Latin Father Tertullian saw the Church in Mary by a juxtaposition of Mary and Eve. For Justin, for example, Mary, acting as God's partner — much as Eve acted as Adam's partner, but, alas, for our spiritual destruction — was instrumental in making a pact of salvation between God and us human beings. By freely cooperating, Mary became Eve's counterpart and the perfect image of the Church in working out the redemption of the human race with Christ in her receptive activity as spouse and mother.

Irenaeus assigns an active role to Mary in the recapitulation by Christ of the whole human race back to God's original plan as children of God. Tertullian linked Eve, Mary, and Church so that both Mary and the Church become the second New Eve. "It comes about that just as Christ was born of a virgin, we also are spiritually reborn of a Virgin cleansed of all spots through Christ. This Virgin is the Church."[3]

From what has been said, we can understand the insights of the early Fathers in linking Mary with the Church and in seeing in both of them the source of universal mediation with Christ the Head. The Church is humanity saved, but it is also that which saves humanity. It is a mediator of salvation, associated with the one Savior, Jesus Christ, in bringing about the recapitulation of the whole created world back to the original plan of God.

The Church is the Savior's representative here on earth. So, too, Mary is the most perfect, the fullest way, the peak of redeemed humanity, but she is also united in the saving of redeemed humanity by being associated with the Savior as a type of the very same saving role exercised by the Church.

The Church is the Mystical Bride of Christ, forming one Body with him in receiving the fruits of his work, his *pleroma*, the fullness of graces. The Church is also the Mystical Mother, giving birth to individual persons through the imparting of divine grace. Mary is the perfect type of the Church, because in her are fulfilled perfect virginal emptiness in complete surrender to God's will and also perfect motherhood. Mary is placed in the center of the economy of salvation, in the center of the Church whose essence is to receive, as virgin-spouse, the fruits of Christ, and to give birth, as mother, to the people of God.

Birthgiver to God

In her total dependence and absolute potential before God in her virginity, Mary cooperates to become literally the *Theotokos,* the Birthgiver to God. In Christian devotion to Mary there has always been a danger of making her divine motherhood a mere physical endowment instead of placing Mary and her self-determination to cooperate with Jesus Christ, the New Adam, into the whole drama of the history of salvation. By returning to the early Fathers of the Church and developing their concept of Mary as the New Eve we can avoid such an error. She will not be a fourth member vying for divinity, but she will be the epitome of all that God has decreed humankind to be through cooperation with God's graces.

Only by keeping in mind what Mary's *fiat* meant in the whole picture of God's merciful condescension to redeem us through Jesus Christ can we truly understand her divine motherhood and also prepare ourselves for a proper veneration of her as our mother and the archetype of what each Christian, each human being created according to God's image and likeness (Gen. 1:26), of what the Universal Church and in potentiality the entire created world should become.

The linking of Mary to Christ in his redemptive act of bringing eternal, divine life to the human race is found in the earliest writings of the Greek Fathers around the theme of the New Adam and the New Eve. St. Justin (d. 165) gives the first development of the parallelism between the two virgins and mothers, Eve and Mary, upon which St. Irenaeus (d. 202) builds his theology of redemption around St. Paul's idea of "recirculation" or "recapitulation."

Both are virgins who give birth, one through disobedience to death, while the other through faith and joy to him who is salvation to the human race. St. Epiphanius (d. 403), perhaps more than all other early Fathers, builds upon Irenaeus's parallelism of the first Eve and the New Eve, both virgins and mothers:

> Eve had been for us an occasion of death and through her, death entered into the World. Mary had been the occasion of life and through her, life had been born in us. It is for this reason that the Son of God has come into the world.... And he came to us precisely through a woman and thus became for us the life.... All this cannot be accomplished absolutely in her [Eve], but it is accomplished in truth in this Seed, holy and chosen absolutely unique which came from Mary and not from any union with man. It is he who came to destroy the power of the dragon.... This is why the Only Begotten came from a woman, to destroy the serpent.[4]

The Fathers' understanding of Mary as the Mother of God and our Mother is never considered except in relation to the parallel between Eve and Mary and between Mary and her Son, the first of a new creation. We can summarize the patristic common teaching by pointing out that in their thinking Eve is a figure, a type of Mary as the first shadowing, imperfect, preparatory for a more nuptial union between God and humanity to be realized in Mary first and then in the Church.[5] Thus the two elements of the first Eve that were restored to their primitive perfection by the second Eve, Mary, and were to be carried out by the third Eve, the Church, are *virgin* and the *mother of the living*.

In patristic literature Mary's maternity is never considered merely as passive, but as an active receptivity of divine life through her faith and obedience to bring Christ to birth, even now in her glorious life, in her active role to participate in the redemption of the human race by mothering Christ anew into the created world.

Mary is given the role of being the archetype of what it means for us human beings to be members in the Church and members of the human race. She is the first one to be redeemed through the merits of Jesus Christ, since grace in her reached such a perfect victory over sin that God's Spirit was working in the most powerful and intimate manner throughout her whole life. Yet Mary always cooperated by giving her free consent to obey the movements of the Spirit.

Not only is Mary archetypical and exemplary of what we must become by imitating her faith, hope, and love, but she is also actively interceding for all of us that the Holy Spirit be poured out abundantly upon us, so we may actually become what she, as the prototype, has always been in her earthly life and now in her glorious oneness with the risen Lord.

Only in the Holy Spirit will we grow in understanding the dynamics of the process of God sending his Spirit, not only upon the virgin of Nazareth, but upon all of us Christians and upon God's entire created world. The heavenly Father is continuously sending his Spirit of love upon us who in union with Mary and all the saints virginally receive his impregnation of his Word within us. Through the same Spirit, we, with Mary, are to become the Mother of Christ as we bring him forth and give him to the world. The microcosm is becoming the macrocosm. The macrocosm is becoming the fulfilled microcosm!

Mary's titles as virgin and mother of God, the Birthgiver to Christ, the incarnate Word of God, are at the heart of devotion of Eastern Christians toward Mary. She is of all God's creatures the most precious, finite gift God has given us. And when the Eastern Christians are at a loss as to what to offer God as a befitting gift for his Son, Jesus Christ, they turn to their heavenly Mother. The beautiful hymn sung at Christmas clearly shows this loving attitude toward Mary:

What shall we bring to Thee, Christ,
who this day has appeared on our earth as man for us?
All Thy other creatures bring something to Thee this day:
angels, heavenly song;
the heavens, the stars;
the Wisemen, gifts;
the shepherds, wonderment;
the earth, a cave;
the desert, a crib;
and we, we offer the Virgin Mother.

CHAPTER ELEVEN

Devotion to Christian Icons

THE GREAT DEVOTION of Eastern Christians to religious icons is an area of piety that is not easily understood by most Western Christians. In the Christian East icons are venerated in the same manner in which we venerate Sacred Scripture. This follows from the constant right teaching about veneration of icons taught by all the great Eastern theologians from the earliest centuries up to the present and universally practiced by all Eastern Christians.

To understand true devotion to icons let us begin with the reality of Christianity that Jesus Christ is the true image or icon (in Greek, *eikon*) of the unseen God (Col. 1:15). Early Christian theologians, who were also persons of deep prayer in oneness with Jesus Christ risen, taught that the law of prayer (*lex orandi*) comes out of the revealed truths which Christians believe in and act upon (*lex credendi*). They evolved an entire Christian incarnational theology from the two basic truths revealed by God in Holy Scripture by focusing especially upon their doctrine of image and likeness.

The first truth all Christians hold is that Jesus Christ is truly God from all eternity. By taking upon himself our material humanity (John 1:14) he becomes the material form and the way we can communicate with the invisible and active presence of the unseen God (Col. 1:15–18). Jesus is the Good News of God's great love for us human beings (John 3:16). We are immersed in matter and in our sinful brokenness in a world that is in bondage to sin and evil forces, impeding our ability to be in loving harmony with God and the created cosmos (Rom. 8:21). We have no way of moving into the invisible presence of the all-transcendent Source of all being, God, Trinity, by our own powers.

But in him, Jesus Christ, the Word made flesh for love of us, we now have the way out of our darkness. He is the "radiant light of God's glory and the perfect copy of his nature" (Heb. 1:3). Who sees him, sees the Father (John 14:9). Thus the second truth is that matter is very good in God's eyes (Gen. 1:31), especially when the Trinity decides to create us human beings out of matter "according to the image and likeness" (Gen. 1:26) that is Jesus Christ. We are to become progressively divinized in Christ Jesus by the workings of Jesus risen and his Holy Spirit as we become more and more made into his likeness by a progressive oneness with him and as we surrender in obedient love to his commands.

We are not the image or icon of God. Only Jesus Christ, God-Man, is the perfect reflection of the eternal God in human, material form. Yet we, alone among all other material beings, can be self-transcendently present to God's spiritual reality and become sharers in his very own divine nature by grace (2 Pet. 1:4).

Icon as Prayer

If God-Trinity is truly present within matter, especially in the
Word incarnate, Jesus Christ, then the whole material world,
starting with our embodied beings, can be our point of communing with the transcendent presence of God, as uncreated
energies of love. If the divine Trinity is actively operating in and
through matter to give themselves to us as Father, Son, and Holy
Spirit, then we should have reverence as we touch God's material
world to find God at the heart of matter.

In Eastern Christianity art and theology go together. They cannot be separated. Both art and theology express the deepest inner
feelings of the heart. Art and theology articulate God's living revelation, but art does it in a visible, plastic way. An icon is a picture
of a sacred subject which is painted on a panel of wood. The surface beneath is prepared with a mixture of powdered alabaster
and glue beneath which linen is sometimes stretched. Colors are
laid on, using the yolk of an egg as medium.

Icon paintings are possible because of the humanity of Christ, a
new humanity which was fully restored to communion with God.
Our humanity was deified in virtue of God becoming truly man,
so that through his Spirit, Jesus could restore in us, his followers,
the image of God unto his likeness. The icon is a concrete instance
of the divine Presence revivifying matter.

The Melkite Catholic Archbishop Joseph Raya well explains
how an icon reflects in itself a microcosmic divinization of what
the entire material cosmos is capable of becoming through Jesus
Christ and his Spirit:

> In an icon, all the elements of nature are represented and
> transformed into a vision of God. The mineral world is rep-
> resented by chalk and alabaster, which is covered by paint
> and by the jewels and precious metals which adorn the icon.
> The plant world is represented by the wood on which the
> icon is painted. The animal world is represented by the egg

with which the paint is mixed. And even the human world is represented by the relics of the saints which are added to the paint. This amalgamation of all the elements of creation in the icon is an assertion of, and emphasis upon, the indwelling holiness of the entire created world which participates and shares in the redemption of Christ.[1]

An icon for Eastern Christians is more than a picture, more than a teacher of truths revealed by God, more than a window to another world. It is, for the believers, an *inscape*, a leading through matter into a fuller participation, or at least experience, of the Incomprehensible One. When one stands before an icon with the right humble dispositions of heart and mind, one is really in touch with the presence of the subject which the icon represents.

St. Basil in the fourth century gave the classical formulation for true veneration of icons: "The honor paid to images passes on to the prototype."[2] A blessed icon, painted according to the traditional rules of the canons on icons, makes it possible for the suppliant to rise through this visible representation of Jesus Christ, Our Lady, or other saints or angels to the spiritual presence of that person. The icon is the place where Christ and the angels and saints appear to us. It is our prayerful meeting point of contact with them. Praying before an icon, we pray directly to Christ and the other heavenly citizens. Kissing the icon, we kiss the person in glory thus represented in the icon. Bowing low before it, we bow before that person.

If such an icon portrays the spiritualized person and the hands and body do not have the proportions of earthlings, it makes little difference. An icon is not a photograph or a realistic image invented by the iconographer. The artist seeks to represent, as far as a graphic medium can, the spirituality of the person in glory. The suppliant kneeling before the icon is moved by the spirituality expressed in the represented person and through this rises to his or her real and glorious presence.

Icon painting is not merely an art, humanly learned. It is a prayer, accompanied by fasting and prayer on the part of the artist. The artist approaches the painting of the icon only after receiving the sacraments of Confession and Communion. God is entreated to use this instrument of the icon and the painter as a channel of grace. The Eastern Ritual gives the following prayer in the ceremony of the blessing of an icon: "O Lord, Our God, send down the grace of your Holy Spirit upon this icon ... bless it and make it holy ... grant to it the power and strength of miraculous deeds. Make it a spring of recovery and healing."

St. John Damascene has written a beautiful treatise on icon devotion in the Eastern Churches. He sums it all up in the words: "What is seen sanctifies our thoughts and so they fly towards the unseen Majesty of God."[3]

The sacramental presence in wood and color and lines is brought about by the prayer of the Church. The connection between the icon and what it depicts is created by the Church. Through the blessing the icon and all the material used in the painting of the image become a link between the human and divine through which the worshiper comes into contact with "the other world." This blessing establishes the connection between the image and the prototype represented. It is a mystical encounter.

Under the visible signs of colors and lines the eyes of faith can unfailingly discern and comprehend the transcendent reality truly present through the power of the Holy Spirit. Through this presence, we coparticipate in the mystery and the Lord is then continually present in his Church, giving it life and healing. Through the icon, we intimately come in touch with God.

The Iconographer

Have you ever prayed in an Eastern Rite church during a liturgical service that unfolded amid numerous icons, especially those of Christ and our Lady on the *iconostasis?* This is the large screen that separates the altar, the symbol of the awesome Holy of Holies, from the people, symbol of God's created world. Or do you possess in your home a favorite icon before which you "center" yourself in the divine presence? The icon, you will soon discover, is never merely a picture, a photocopy of a sense reality as perceived by the artist. Icons transcend the limits of other forms of art because of their symbolical meaning for the religious community at prayer.

The value of an icon lies, not in the art itself, but in the artist, the iconographer. The reason lies in the fact that he or she must be a holy, prayerful "theologian," in vital, living touch with the orthodox teachings of the Church, discovered through fasting, ascetical purity of the heart, and prayer that is "incessant" in the heart.

Eastern iconographers seek to give to the icons they paint an abstract and hieratic or sacred character. Just as the power of the Holy Spirit shone forth from the transfigured Christ on Mount Tabor, so also the human figures radiate a divine awareness, with the gold background of icons representing the grace of the Holy Spirit.

Transfiguration of Matter

One cannot understand the sacredness of icons and, therefore, the possibility of veneration through the materiality of the icons paid to the person represented in the icons without having recourse to the working of the Holy Spirit. It is a gift of the Spirit that allows the painter to paint in the sacred manner of "incarnating" again the presence of Christ and the saints and angels. The same gift allows the faithful praying before such icons to be swept up into the living presence of Christ and his saints and angels.

The Christian's participation in the spiritual transfiguration of matter into an icon, or symbol of faith, be it active (on the part of the painter or passive (that of the believer), brings to the Christian an experience of divinization. The agent of such divinization is always the Holy Spirit.

The icon is an example of the transfiguration of matter by the divine Spirit and by human beings. The divine Spirit by breathing a living spirit into the first man, made him and the first woman according to God's image and likeness (Gen. 1:26–27). Now Christian artists and believers, praying before such icons, take matter and, through their spiritual powers in collaboration with God's Spirit, make icons of Christ or of God-like images of saints and, in prayer, summon Christ and the saints into their history to lead the faithful into the transfigured world of heaven.

The transfigured quality of both the icon and the person of faith anticipates and indicates the ultimate transfiguration which is yet to come in its fullness when the entire cosmos will be transfigured by the power of God in his Spirit of love, who is "all in all" (1 Cor. 15:28). As you pray before such Eastern icons, they become a medium that manifests in prayer Christ, all human beings in Christ, and the whole cosmos in the perspective of the transfiguration into Christ, by the Holy Spirit. The Holy Spirit transfigures us into the icon or likeness of Jesus Christ.

If Christ, the transfigured, risen Lord, can be so close to us and, in matter, can be constantly experienced as more intimate to us than we are to ourselves, then why should we ever fear?

CHAPTER TWELVE

The Holy Spirit: Gift of Love

HAT WE ARE SEEING in our modern technological world and in our own individual lives is a crying out almost in desperation to discover ourselves as unique, beautiful, joyful persons who feel themselves worthwhile and loved by others. Through our hyperactivity and the depersonalization brought about by our technological world, all of us desire a greater sense of our personhood and individuation in our relationships with one another, with God, and with the world around us.

145

Western organized religions, which tend toward teachings and dogmas, hierarchical structures of authority and liturgical ritualism are finding a need to revitalize themselves. The faithful are in search of transcendence and intimate, immanent, personal encounters with a living God. This God truly loves them and transforms their brokenness and darkness into new, loving creativity to help cocreate with God a better society that reflects the immanent presence of the living Trinity in all of creation.

Most Christian theologians, both of the Eastern and Western Churches, generally complain that preachers and parishioners tend to neglect the importance of the Holy Spirit in Christian piety. No doubt this is due to the modern technological tendency to objectivize the spiritual world, including the Trinity.

What is greatly needed to revitalize the importance of the Holy Spirit is to learn from the early Eastern Christian mystics and theologians their mystical and apophatic approach to the Holy Spirit. These early Eastern Fathers approached the Holy Spirit, not only in the apophatic symbols found to describe the Spirit in both the Old and New Testaments, but also and most importantly they developed their teaching, not as an independent doctrine, but always in the context of their teachings on Christ, the Holy Trinity, redemption, grace, and the ascetical life.

It is interesting to note that only after the early Fathers had valiantly fought the heresies of Arianism, Nestorianism, and Monophysitism did St. Athanasius in his *Letters to Serapion,* St. Basil in his *On the Holy Spirit,* and St. Cyril of Alexandria in his *Commentary on the Gospel of St. John* write the three most important patristic writings on the Holy Spirit. Because of their use of the scriptural symbols that referred to the Holy Spirit and their apophatic, mystical approach to the Trinity, the Orthodox and other Eastern Christian Churches have relied principally on these three works as the essential teaching on the subject of the Holy Spirit.

The Spirit of God

As was pointed out in chapter 3, "apophaticism" is a key term among the mystical writers of the Christian East. This was especially evident in the writings of St. Athanasius, St. Basil, and St. Cyril of Alexandria on the Holy Spirit. They were very aware that in writing about the Holy Spirit there was a need to seek a "higher" form of knowledge than the *cataphatic,* or positive, knowledge available through human reasoning.

Some things that they wrote about God the Trinity and the Holy Spirit specifically may be understood in some manner through discursive knowledge. Yet in another manner they saw that such knowledge was inadequate with regard to the mystical role of the Spirit in relation to the Trinity with regard to the mission of the Spirit in the created world and in the economy of salvation. Thus they saw the *apophatic* element to be more applicable than a mere negation in the area of human linguistics. Its essential characteristic was always positive and was to be experienced as Christians opened themselves to the release of the Holy Spirit in their daily lives.

Such knowledge is a real knowing that is a gifted experience in love by God-Trinity. God gifts the humble and pure of heart with such knowledge, always as a work of the Holy Spirit. This is clearly highlighted by Basil in his treatise *On the Holy Spirit*:

> If we are illumined by divine power, and fix our eyes on the beauty of the image of the invisible God, and through the image are led up to the indescribable beauty of its source, it is because we have been inseparably joined to the Spirit of knowledge. He gives those who love the vision of truth the power which enables them to see the image, and this power is himself. He does lead them to knowledge personally. "No one knows the Father except the Son" (Matt. 11:27), and "No one can say 'Jesus is Lord' except in the Holy Spirit" (1 Cor. 12:3).[1]

We have no way of knowing the Father but through the Son. In Jesus Christ we not only see the perfect human expression of the eternal Word-Son of the Father, but we also see the image of the Godhead, as it moves eternally to express its fullness in love to his Son. The Father must be in his imaged-Word. The Word has meaning only because he is the exact image of the Father who is communicating himself in his Word. The Father knows himself only in his image, his Son. The Godhead concentrates his entire essence in the Son, who allows the Father to become the knower and the Son to become known and vice versa. The Son in the Spirit is the knower as he knows the Father to be his total Source and Origin of being and thus the Father is known as Father.

This interrelationship between the Father and Son in self-knowledge cannot be possible except through the Holy Spirit, and that is why, as the Eastern Fathers universally affirmed, that there must be a triple movement within the one Godhead. It is the Holy Spirit who eternally illumines the mystery for the Father and the Son.

The Father and Son mutually know themselves and love themselves through self-giving to each other through the Holy Spirit who is the binding gift of love between the Father and the Son.

Thus the Holy Spirit cannot be an accidental relation, a "thing" produced, even from all eternity, but must be in a mysterious, uncreated manner the one that unites the Father and Son eternally in love that cannot be separated from the knowing of the Father in his Son. The Spirit makes it possible for the unity of the Godhead to be shared without destroying that unity in the diversity of the three divine persons who share in that same essence.

From this threefold movement, therefore, flows all reality within the Trinity and also within the created order of God's shared being through his uncreated energies of love. The divine Logos is the natural and perfect expression of the Father and is naturally and perfectly expressed by the love of the Father that is the Spirit. Knowledge is not enough; it must be completed by love since it exists in that first movement of self-giving. Love completes knowledge, and, although knowledge and love are not the same, within the Trinity the Son is known in the love of the Father. Knowing the Father in his returned love can be possible only through "realized love," which is the Spirit proceeding from the Father and radiating the Son back to the Father. Yet both the Son and Spirit proceed differently from the one and same Source, the Father.

If there were only the Father and the Son, there would be no community of two persons giving themselves to each other and fructifying a third in an *I-Thou-We* community. There would be no movement outside of a mutual desire toward *union*. The result would be not only a denial of the Trinity, but a negation of a God who has so loved us as to give us his only begotten Son so that in his gift, the Spirit of love, we might have eternal life (John 3:16).

True love is driven to a transcendence that wants love received to be shared by a third person. The Son wants to love the Father with a perfect mutual love just as the Father loves him.[2] It would be an imperfection between the Father and the Son if their love did not want to be shared with a third. To share this mutual love there is need of a loved one that is loved equally as the Father loves the Son and the Son loves the Father. This is the Holy Spirit.[3]

Thus the Holy Spirit must find his uniqueness as the personalized act of love coming out of the mutual love of the Father and Son, loving each other in their mutual gift of love, their Holy Spirit. His being as a person within the Trinity consists in being the act of union and distinction between the Father and Son, and in this "action" the Spirit finds his *personhood*. Thus the Spirit can never be considered apart from either the Father or the Son.

Our Christian faith assures us from the Old and New Testament revelations that God, as a trinitarian community of love, explodes in their *kenotic,* or self-emptying, love to create a world of seemingly infinite diversity. Yet all multiplicity is continually being guided by the loving, overshadowing Holy Spirit to fashion a oneness, the fullness of the Logos-God, enfleshed in matter. The Spirit is moving throughout the material world, lovingly drawing God's embryonic creation into the definitive unity, as was expressed in chapter 9.

St. Athanasius in the fourth century expressed such Christian optimism in a world moving toward beauty and harmony through the working of the Holy Spirit:

> Like a musician who has attuned his lyre, and by artistic blending of low and high and medium tones produces a single melody, so the Wisdom of God, holding the universe like a lyre, adapting things heavenly to things earthly, and earthly things to heavenly, harmonizes them all, and leading them by his will, makes one world-order in beauty and harmony.[4]

God the Father utters his creative Word by calling his Spirit down upon the cosmos in a continuous cosmic *epiklesis,* which means in Greek a calling down upon something, to divinize matter into spirit. God in the Old Testament and also in the New breathes his breath, his *ruah,* his loving Spirit, as the principle of life into all his creation. The beasts of the land are sustained by his breath. The heavens are also the work of God's enspiriting breath, his Spirit (Gen. 7:15).

In a special way God breathes his breath into man and woman and they become human persons, made in God's own image and likeness (Gen. 1:26–27). All of us human beings, by the inbreathing of God's Spirit, are called to cooperate in harmonizing all of creation into a work of conscious love, a harmony of diversity in oneness through love (Gen. 1:28–30).

A universal statement repeated by all the Eastern Fathers concerning the gift of the Holy Spirit is that the Logos incarnated came into this world as totally human in order that we human beings might become God by grace.[5]

Jesus Reveals to Us the Spirit

We see, therefore, that the Spirit has always been working together with the Logos as the power of God's love to actuate and harmonize the potentialities locked into the trinitarian creation of all material creatures. The Spirit, as we see in the Gospel account of the annunciation of the Good News that would bring about a New Creation, "overshadowed" Mary and made her a temple for the real Ark of the Covenant, Jesus Christ. The Word incarnate comes to lead us from sin through forgiveness and prompt our acceptance of God's mercy. He is the way for the "imperfect" to become holy and sinless.

Once the Word becomes flesh it is Jesus Christ, the Word and Son of the Father incarnate out of love for us, who brings us into the awesome mystery of the Trinity as a communion in its own life through his revealing Holy Spirit.

To the risen Jesus it has been given by the Father to bestow upon us the power and glory of God's Spirit. This Spirit of perfect love could not be given to us until Jesus had freely died for us (John 7:39). He promised to send us the Holy Spirit as a Paraclete, consoler and advocate, a help to us, so that we could live forever in our new oneness with the risen Lord and his eternal Father that the Spirit would bring about. "It is for your own good that I am going because unless I go, the Advocate will not come to you but if I do go, I will send him to you" (John 16:7).

A unique insight of great originality is given by St. Athanasius, as we already mentioned. It is the role of the Holy Spirit, sent into our hearts by the Father and the Son (Rom. 5:5), to perfect what the Son has made possible by divinizing us into loving children of the heavenly Father (Rom. 8:15–16). Athanasius writes:

The Son is in the Spirit and in his own image just as the Father is in the Son.[6]

The Spirit has been called and is really the Image of the Son.... Since therefore they [the heretics, especially the

Pneumatomachoi] hold that the Son is not a creature; his image cannot either be a creature.

For, as such is the Image, so such must necessarily be he of whom he is the Image.[7]

It is clear that he is not a creature who is not absolutely of the nature of angels who are fallible, but who is the Image of the Son and he the Image of the Father.[8]

The Son is the Image of the invisible God and the Spirit is the Image of the Son.[9]

St. John, the beloved disciple of Jesus, cannot get over the miracle of our regeneration, our rebirth, not by water alone, but by the Holy Spirit (John 3:3, 5). "Think of the love that the Father has lavished on us by letting us be called God's children; and that is what we are" (1 John 3:1). St. Paul describes the main work of the Spirit as bringing us into a new life, a life in Jesus which regenerates us into true children of God: "The Spirit of God has made his home in you ... and if the Spirit of him who raised Jesus from the dead is living in you, then he who raised Jesus from the dead will give life to your own mortal bodies through his Spirit living in you" (Rom. 8:9, 11).

God's very own Spirit dwells within us as in his temple (1 Cor. 6:19–20). We possess through the Spirit the fullness of the triune God living and acting in love within us at all times during our waking and sleeping hours. This Spirit of love brings new life to its fullness to the extent that we allow the Spirit to become our Guide, Teacher, and Revealer, as he guides us Christians to make choices according to the mind of Christ.

Jesus is the perfect Image of the invisible God (Col. 1:15), especially as he, who was one with God from all eternity, did not deem it an honor to hold on to his divinity, but he "emptied" (*kenosis*, the act of self-emptying) himself by freely dying for us human beings (Phil. 2:6–7). If the Holy Spirit is the perfect Image of the Son, how does the Spirit image the Son? Jesus promised that the work of the Spirit would be "to teach you everything and to call to your mind all that I have said to you" (John 14:26). The imaging by the Spirit of Jesus Christ is the total self-emptying love that constitutes the Spirit's uniqueness within the Trinity and in his unique activities in the economy of salvation. He witnesses to the first Apostles and through their faith to future Christians that Jesus is truly *Lord* and *Master*, which for St. Paul is a confession of faith in the divinity of Jesus, one with the Father through the Spirit.

The Spirit witnesses to the living presence of the risen Jesus and makes him present among the members of Christ's Body, the Church, living intimately within the individual Christian (John 14:23). The same Spirit in his self-emptying as perfect gift of love images Christ's humility; the Spirit hides himself as an independent entity who lives to exalt the Father and the Son in glory and power and love. The Spirit has no "face" or identity except by being poured love that is his personhood in action as he lives to serve the revelation of the Father and the Son through the hidden love that unites us with the Father and Son. In a miracle of miracles, the Spirit lives as true love must, to bring forth the uniqueness of each Christian member in the Body of Christ.

Our Divinization by the Holy Spirit

St. Symeon the New Theologian (d. 1022), one of the greatest mystics of the Eastern Churches,[10] although he never wrote a complete treatise on the Holy Spirit as did Athanasius and Basil, added a new dimension to our understanding. He shows originality in boldly teaching the need which he sees grounded in Holy Scripture, not only of a baptism of water, but also an added stage in the Christian's life which he calls the *baptism in the Holy Spirit*. He is careful to point out that the Christian's first baptism truly confers grace with the indwelling of the Holy Trinity, Father, Son, and Holy Spirit. Yet there is still a fuller possession of the Spirit

that comes through a deeper faith. This infusion of faith by the
Holy Spirit comes about only through life's trials and tribulations
that challenge us to turn in repentance to the Lord as Savior and
Healer. He writes:

> In holy baptism we receive remission of our faults; we have
> been delivered from the ancient curse; we are sanctified by
> the presence of the Holy Spirit. But the perfect grace accord-
> ing to the promise: "I will dwell in them and walk among
> them" (2 Cor. 6:16), we have not yet received for it is the
> inheritance of the faithful confirmed in the faith who have
> tested their faith by their works.[11]

For Symeon the important question posed to baptized Christians is not whether the Holy Spirit lives within us, but whether
we are *consciously* aware of the Holy Spirit through a penitential
conversion that must be a continued process.

Symeon conceives the operations of the Holy Spirit in us in a
twofold manner: one, divinizing us to become truly children of
God by grace and adoption, and the other, the continued process of sanctification, especially by means of illumination and
revelation.

Using patristic language, Symeon over and over comes back to
his fixed formula that the Holy Spirit regenerates us, making us
children of God, gods by adoption, by "disposition and grace":

> The adoption through regeneration is due to the Holy Spirit
> who makes us become gods by disposition and grace [in
> Greek: *thesei kai chariti*], who makes us to be called heirs
> of God and coheirs with Christ... whereby we see God and
> Christ himself living in us according to his divinity and
> moving around in a conscious [*gnostos*] manner within us.[12]

Symeon insists on the need for personal illumination by the
Holy Spirit to understand Holy Scripture. Then in the light of the
interior message that God reveals through his Holy Spirit, we are
able to know the commandments, i.e., the will of God concretized

in daily life. The Holy Spirit makes it possible to become children of light, but also for us to live lives as individual and unique children of God. The Holy Spirit vivifies us. He is our food and our drink. He it is who transforms bread and wine into the Body and Blood of Christ.[13] But when we experience the grace of the Holy Spirit covering ourselves with clear knowledge, we know that we have put on Jesus Christ.[14]

The Spirit of God is called "Holy" in Scripture. As all three persons in the Trinity are spirit, so all three are holy. God is holy in his self-giving love of himself to us in and through the Holy Spirit. God's holiness is seen as he gives himself to us as a gift of love so we can truly participate in his very nature (2 Pet. 1:4). In this very holy union, there is diversity of unique personhood of ourselves and each member of the Trinity. In their uncreated energies, distinct from the one essence of God that is totally incomprehensible by us, they give themselves to us freely. This is the work of the Holy Spirit, who gives us new illumination and knowledge beyond our mere natural understanding; we are called to live in an ecstatic union within the Trinity of the *I* and the *Thou* and the *We*. The work of the Holy Spirit is to bring us into God's holiness, and thus we become holy as our Father and Jesus Christ are holy.

St. Cyril of Alexandria well summarizes the doctrine of the Eastern Fathers concerning the work of the Holy Spirit. He teaches that the Spirit is the bond of union which binds us to the Son and Father. The Spirit is the image of the Son and consequently the image of the Father. He is the sanctifying power of the divinity. Sanctity is as essential to the Holy Spirit as paternity is to the Father and filiation is to the Son.[15]

Perhaps the best summation of what we have written here on the apophatic nature of the Holy Spirit can be found in one of St. Symeon the New Theologian's *Hymns to Divine Love:*

Being God, the Divine Spirit refashions completely those whom he receives within himself.

He makes them completely anew.

He renews them in an amazing manner.

So likewise the Divine Spirit, incorruptible, gives incorruptibility.

Being immortal, he gives immortality.

Because he is light that never sets,

he transforms all of them into light in whom he comes down
and dwells.

And because he is life, he bestows life to all.

As he is of the same nature as Christ, being of the same
essence as well as the same in glory,

and being united with him, he forms them absolutely similar
to Christ.

...He is our Benefactor

and he wishes that all of us become what he himself is....

Therefore, as you wisely understand this,

hasten to receive the Spirit, who comes from God and is
divine,

in order...to become heirs of the heavenly Kingdom forever.[16]

Epilogue

E HAVE CALLED THIS "a journey" into the specialized world of Eastern Christian spirituality. There are all sorts of journeys we take. The Israelites journeyed for forty years through the desert, and only the faithful "Anawim," the "poor in spirit," entered into the promised land. Their long nomadic journey ended and yielded to a deeper journey into their hearts as they lived out their commitment to God's *hesed* covenant.

Yet there is a danger in describing this book as a journey. Our experiences of taking a journey usually are tied to a linear movement from one place to another, always coming back to our beginning base. The impression is often given that after a journey we are now back "to business as usual," as though we had not been away.

It is my humble hope that this journey back into the writings of some of the leading Eastern Fathers of the early eight centuries will continue throughout your life. Such a journey will deepen in richness as you grow in the vibrancy of such spiritual views of these Eastern Christian theologians and mystics. May these teachings foster in your personal life a deeper gratitude to God for the treasures locked in the patristic writings of the Eastern Fathers.

I would like to conclude this work by quoting from St. Gregory of Nyssa:

> We who among beings count for nothing, who are dust, grass, vanity, who have been adopted to be children of the God of the universe, become the friend of this Being of such excellence and grandeur. This is a mystery that we can neither see nor understand nor comprehend. What thanks should we give for so great a favor? What word, what thought, what lifting up of mind in order to exalt the superabundance of this grace? We surpass our own very nature.
>
> From mortal beings we become immortal, from perishable beings we become imperishable. From ephemeral we become eternal. In a word, from human beings we become gods.
>
> In fact, rendered worthy to become children of God, we will have in ourselves the dignity of the Father, enriched by all the inheritance of the goods of the Father.
>
> O munificence of the Lord, so bountiful. . . . How great are the gifts of such ineffable treasures![1]

Notes

Preface

(Note: Translations of passages in Greek, Latin, Old Slavonic, and the modern languages in which certain cited works have been used, such as German, French, and Italian, have usually been made by myself. For other texts cited permission has been sought and granted for passages of more than two or three paragraphs.)

1. John T. Chirban, "Developmental Stages in Orthodox Christianity," in *Transformations of Consciousness,* ed. K. Wilber, J. Engler, and D. P. Brown (Boston and London: New Science Library, Shambhala, 1986), 296ff.

Chapter One / The Holy Trinity: Mysticism of Community

1. Søren Kierkegaard, *The Sickness unto Death,* trans. Walter Lowrie (Garden City, N.Y.: Doubleday, 1954), 10.
2. Karl Rahner, *The Trinity,* trans. J. Donceel, S.J. (New York: Herder & Herder, 1969), 10–11.
3. Gregory Nazianzus, *Homilia XLII,* 15; in J. P. Migne, ed., Patrologia Graeca (Paris, 1844; henceforth PG), 36, 476.
4. Friedrich Nietzsche, *The Portable Nietzsche* (New York: Viking, 1954), 12.
5. For a more detailed presentation of the personal divine relationships within the Trinity, see my two books, *Invaded by God* (Denville, N.J.: Dimension Books, 1979) and *God's Community of Love* (Hyde Park, N.Y.: New City Press, 1995).
6. Gabriel Marcel, *Metaphysical Journal,* trans. Bernard Wall (Chicago: H. Regnery Co., 1952), 26, 147, 221.
7. Hilary of Poitiers, *The Trinity,* trans. Stephen McKenna, C.SS.R., The Fathers of the Church 25 (Washington, D.C.: Catholic University Press, 1954), bk. 2, 6; 41.

8. See Otto Michel, "Oikonomia," *Theological Dictionary of the New Testament,* vol. 5, ed. Gerhard Friedrich, trans. G. W. Bromiley (Grand Rapids: Eerdmans Co., 1995), 157–59.

9. Vladimir Lossky, *The Mystical Theology of the Eastern Church* (Naperville, Ill.: Clarke Ltd., 1957), 71.

10. Rahner, *The Trinity,* 22.

11. Ibid., 101.

12. St. Irenaeus, *Adversus Haereses,* bk. V, ch. 28, 4, The Ante-Nicene Fathers 1, ed. A. Roberts and J. Donaldson (Grand Rapids: Eerdmans, 1958), 557.

Chapter Two / Made in God's Image and Likeness

1. Richard Bach, *Jonathan Livingston Seagull* (New York: Macmillan Co., 1970), 90–91.

2. Emil Brunner, *Man in Revolt* (London, 1953), 97–98.

3. Cyril of Alexandria, *Comment. in Joan.* IV, I; PG 74; 316A.

4. See I. Hausherr, S.J., "Dogme et spiritualité orientale," in *Revue d'ascetique et mystique* (1947): 31–33.

5. *Ad Olympium Monachum,* PG 46; 256B.

6. *Adv. oppugn. vitae monasticae,* III, 15; PG 47; 372.

7. St. Irenaeus, *De perfecta Christiani forma,* PG 46; 251–56. St. Athanasius, *Contra Arianos;* 59; PG 26; 273.

8. Irenaeus, *Adversus Haereses,* V, ch. 9; 534. Quotations from Irenaeus are from The Ante-Nicene Fathers 1, ed. A. Roberts, and J. Donaldson (Grand Rapids: Eerdmans, 1962), unless otherwise noted. Quotations used with permission.

9. Epiphanius, *Haereses,* bk. III, t. 1; PG 42; 341–45.

Chapter Three / Luminous Darkness: The Apophatic Way

1. Cyprian Kern, "Les elements de la théologie de Grégoire Palamas," in *Irenikon* 20 (1947): 9.

2. Vladimir Lossky, *Vision of God* (Clayton, Wis.: Faith Press, 1963), 71, 74.

3. St. Gregory of Nyssa, *Comm. on Canticle of Canticles,* PG 44; 1001B.

4. *Contra Eunomium,* XII; PG 45; 940D.

5. Ibid., 941B.

6. *Comm. on Cant. of Canticles,* PG 44; 1000D.

7. See L. Bouyer, *The Spirituality of the New Testament and the Fathers* (New York: Desclée, 1960), 356.

8. Gregory of Nyssa, *On Perfection*, trans. Virginia Woods Callahan, in *Ascetical Works of Gregory of Nyssa*, The Fathers of the Church 58 (Washington, D.C.: Catholic University of America, 1963), 122.

9. *The Life of Moses*, PG 44; 3397D–405A.

10. *Comm. on Cant. of Canticles;* PG 44; 1031B.

11. *Life of Moses*, PG 44; 405A–D.

12. Ibid., 397D–405A.

13. For the complete text in English, see *The Divine Names and the Mystical Theology*, trans. C. E. Rolt (London: SPCK, 1920).

14. Vladimir Lossky, *The Mystical Theology of the Eastern Church* (Naperville, Ill.: Clarke Ltd., 1957), 43.

15. Cited in ibid., 214.

16. The feast of the Epiphany, Matins, Canon 9.

17. *Hirmos* of the Eastern Service of the Byzantine Rite, attributed to St. John Damascene, cited from *Byzantine Daily Worship*, ed. Archbishop Joseph Raya and J. DaVinck (Allendale, N.J.: Alleluia Press, 1973), 855.

18. John Meyendorff, *A Study of Gregory Palamas*, trans. George Lawrence (London: Faith Press, 1964), 131.

19. Basil Krivoshein, "The Ascetical and Theological Teaching of Gregory Palamas," *Eastern Churches Quarterly* 3 (1938–39): 72.

20. Lossky, *The Mystical Theology*, 116.

21. Krivoshein, "The Ascetical and Theological Teaching of Gregory Palamas," 145.

Chapter Four / A Logos Mysticism

1. C. T. Wood, *The Life, Letters and Religion of St. Paul* (Edinburgh: T. & T. Clark, 1925), 320.

2. See Vladimir Lossky, *The Mystical Theology of the Eastern Church* (Naperville, Ill.: Clarke Ltd., 1957), 98.

3. Polycarp Sherwood, *The Earlier Ambigua of St. Maximus the Confessor* (Rome: Herder, 1955), 176.

4. Maximus, *Ambigua;* PG 91; 1308.

5. See J. Pegon, *Centuries sur la Charité de S. Maxime Le Confesseur*, Sources Chrétiennes 9 (Paris: Editions du Cerf, 1943), 54.

6. *Mystagogia;* PG 91; 665–68.

7. See *Ad Thallasium;* PG 90, 63; 673C.

8. *Ambigua*, 5; PG 91; 1060A.

9. See Lossky, *The Mystical Theology*, 146.

Chapter Five / God's Uncreated Energies of Love

1. St. Basil, *Epistle to Eustathius,* quoted by G. Habra, "The Patristic Sources of the Doctrine of Gregory Palamas on the Divine Energies," *Eastern Churches Quarterly* 12 (1957–58): 298.

2. Basil, *Epistle to Ampholochius,* cited by Habra, "The Patristic Sources," 300.

3. Habra, "The Patristic Sources," 296.

4. St. Gregory of Nyssa, *Against Eunomius,* XII, in Habra, "The Patristic Sources," 300.

5. Pseudo-Dionysius, *Celestial Hierarchy,* PG, Vol. III, 1.

6. *The Divine Names and the Mystical Theology,* trans. C. E. Rolt (London: SPCK, 1920), 1.

7. Ibid., *Mystical Theology,* 1.

8. Ibid., *Divine Names, II.*

9. Vladimir Lossky, *The Mystical Theology of the Eastern Church* (Naperville, Ill.: Clarke Ltd., 1957), 1.

10. *Divine Names,* 2.

11. Ibid., 1.

12. J. Meyendorff, *A Study of Gregory Palamas,* trans. George Lawrence (London: Faith Press, 1964), 210.

13. J. Meyendorff, *Grégoire Palamas: Les Triads pour la defense des saints Hésychastes,* 3 vols. (Louvain: Spicilegium Sacrum Lovaniense, 1959), 2:24.

14. Meyendorff, *A Study,* 221–22.

15. See: George Maloney, S.J., *The Mystic of Fire and Light: St. Symeon the New Theologian* (Denville, N.J.: Dimension Books, 1975), 71–72.

16. *Triads,* III, 1, 29.

17. *Against Akindynos,* II, 9.

18. St. Gregory of Nyssa, *Christian Mode of Life,* The Fathers of the Church 58 (Washington, D.C.: Catholic University of America, 1963), 130.

19. Basil Krivoshein, "The Ascetical and Theological Teaching of Gregory Palamas," *The Eastern Churches Quarterly* 3 (1938–39): 28.

20. St. Gregory of Nyssa, *On the Beatitudes,* 7; PG 44; 1280C.

21. *Triads,* III, I, 35.

22. St. Symeon the New Theologian, "Hymn 25," *Hymns of Divine Love,* trans. G. A. Maloney, S.J. (Denville, N.J.: Dimension Books, 1975), 135–36.

23. *St. Symeon the New Theologian: Chapitres théologiques, gnostiques et pratiques,* Sources Chrétiennes 51 (Paris: Cerf, 1968), 2, 17.

Chapter Six / Paradise Lost

1. Vladimir Lossky, *The Mystical Theology of the Eastern Church* (Naperville, Ill.: Clarke Ltd., 1957), 78.
2. Basil, *Quod Deus non est auctor mali,* 6; PG 36; 345B.
3. Ibid.
4. Basil, *Epistola* 233, in A Select Library of Nicene and Post-Nicene Fathers of the Christian Church (Grand Rapids: Eerdmans, 1953), 5:273.
5. *Quod Deus non est...,* 344B.
6. Ibid.
7. Irenaeus, *Adversus Haereses,* ch. 39, 3; 523.
8. Athanasius, *De Incarnatione,* in A Select Library of Nicene and Post-Nicene Fathers of the Christian Church 7:38.
9. Ibid., *Contra Arianos,* III, 33, 412.
10. PG 82; 100.

Chapter Seven / Weep: There Is No Other Way

1. A saying attributed to Abbot Poemen, *Apophthegmata Patrum;* PG 65; 353A.
2. *Ad Demetrium monachum de compunctione;* PG 47; 392–410; *Ad Stelechium de Compunctione,* ibid., 411–22.
3. John Climacus, *The Ladder of Divine Ascent,* trans. Archimandrite Lazarus Moore (London: Faber & Faber, 1959), 114.
4. I. Hausherr, S.J., *Les leçons d'un contemplatif; le traité de l'oraison d'Evagre le Pontique* (Paris: Cerf, 1960), 19.
5. Climacus, Step 7, in *The Ladder of Divine Ascent,* 116.
6. Ibid., 115.
7. See M. Lot-Borodine, "Le mystère du 'don des larmes' " in *La Vie Spirituelle* 48, S. (1936): 65–110.
8. Nilus, *Epistola III;* PG 79; 512D–513B.
9. St. Dorotheus, *Doctrina IV,* no. 5, 6; PG 88; 1665.
10. Gregory Nazianzus, *Oratio XII,* cited by Hausherr, *Penthos, La doctrine de la compunction dans L'Orient chrétien,* in Orientalia Christiana Analecta 144 (Rome: Pontifical Oriental Institute, 1955), 114.
11. P. Tillich, "The Eternal Now," in *The Modern Vision of Death,* ed. N. A. Scott, Jr. (Richmond, Va., 1967), 103.
12. See note 1 above.
13. Climacus, Step 7, in *The Ladder of Divine Ascent,* 116.

Chapter Eight / Praxis: The Ascetical Life

1. See C. A. Van Peursen, *Body, Soul, Spirit: A Survey of the Body-Mind Problem* (London: Oxford University Press, 1966).
2. Symeon the New Theologian, *The Discourses,* trans. C. J. Catanzaro (New York: Paulist Press, 1980), 68–69.
3. Isaac of Sinai; PG 86A, 886B.
4. See Climacus, *Ladder,* PG 88, Step 15; 896D.
5. Evagrius, *To Anatolius: On Eight Thoughts,* in *Philokalia: Early Fathers,* trans. Kadloubovsky and Palmer (London: Faber & Faber, 1954), 110.
6. Maximus the Confessor, *Ambigua,* PG 91; 1081D.
7. Pseudo-Macarius, "Homily 40," in *Intoxicated with God: The Spiritual Homilies of Pseudo-Macarius,* trans G. A. Maloney, S.J. (Denville, N.J.: Dimension Books, 1978), 253.
8. Climacus, *Step 29,* PG 88; 1147 ff.
9. John Cassian, *On the Holy Fathers of Sketis and on Discrimination,* in Palmer et al., *The Philokalia: Early Fathers,* 95–96.
10. Irenaeus, *Adversus Haereses,* V, 6, 531.
11. Maximus the Confessor, *Ambigua;* PG 91; 1305C–1308C.

Chapter Nine / Jesus Christ: The Savior of the World

1. Constantine N. Tsirpanlis, *Introduction to Eastern Patristic Thought and Orthodox Theology* (Collegeville, Minn.: Liturgical Press, 1991), 61.
2. Irenaeus, *Adversus Haereses,* V, 16; PG 7; 1167C.
3. Ibid., I, 19; PG 7; 939B.
4. Gustave Molwitz in his Latin work *Irenaei Potestate* (Dresden, 1874) is the first scholar to treat of the meaning of *anakephalaiosis*. He points out that the word does not come from *kephale,* meaning "head." He insists the word comes from *kephalaion,* meaning the chief point or summary, the whole containing the parts.
5. *Adversus Haereses,* V, 21, 1; 548–49.
6. Ibid., 567.
7. Gregory Nazianzus, *Epistola ad Cledonium;* PG 38; 181.
8. *Oratio 38, 13;* 349.
9. *Oratio 7* (Panegyric to his brother, Caesarius), in A Select Library of Nicene and Post-Nicene Fathers of the Christian Church, 23:237.
10. *Life of Moses,* Sources Chrétiennes 6 (Paris: Cerf, 1941), 98.
11. Gregory Nyssa, *De Opif. Hom.,* 16, 16, 406, in A Select Library of Nicene and Post-Nicene Fathers of the Christian Church.
12. *De Virginitate;* PG 46; 370B.

13. *De Oratione cat. magna,* in A Select Library of Nicene and Post-Nicene Fathers of the Christian Church 25:495.

14. Ibid., 26:489.

15. P. Sherwood, *St. Maximus the Confessor: The Ascetic Life and the Four Centuries on Charity,* in Ancient Christian Writers 21 (Westminster, Md.: Newman, 1955), 5.

16. Maximus, *Capita Theologica et Oeconomica;* PG 90; 1108A–B.

17. Maximus, *The Earlier Ambigua,* trans. Polycarp Sherwood (Rome: Herder, 1955), 5–6.

18. *St. Maximus the Confessor: The Ascetic Life and the Four Centuries on Charity,* I, 95; in Ancient Christian Writers 151.

19. *Relatio Motionis;* PG 90; 124A.

20. *Quaest. ad Thal.;* PG 90; 381B.

21. *Mystagogia;* PG 91; 665–68.

22. Vladimir Lossky, *The Mystical Theology of the Eastern Church* (Naperville, Ill.: Clarke Ltd., 1957), 111.

Chapter Ten / Mary: Microcosm of a New Creation

1. For a detailed explanation of archetype, see Beverly Moon, "Archetypes," in *The Encyclopedia of Religions* (New York: Macmillan Co., 1987), 1:379–82.

2. H. Semmelroth, S.J., *Mary-Church* (New York: Sheed & Ward, 1966), 32.

3. Quoted by H. Koch, *Virgo Eva–Virgo Maria* (Berlin and Leipzig, 1937), 42.

4. St. Epiphanius, *Panarion LXVIII,* ch. 18–19; PG 42; 733 ff.

5. For detailed texts, see my book *Mary: The Womb of God* (Denville, N.J.: Dimension Books, 1976), esp. 56–69.

Chapter Eleven / Devotion to Christian Icons

1. Archbishop Joseph Raya, *The Face of God* (Denville, N.J.: Dimension Books, 1976), 153.

2. St. Basil, PG 32; 149.

3. St. John Damascene, *On Holy Images,* trans. Mary H. Alliec (London: Thomas Baker, 1898), 22.

Chapter Twelve / The Holy Spirit: Gift of Love

1. St. Basil, *On the Holy Spirit* (Crestwood, N.Y.: St. Vladimir's Seminary Press, 1980), nos. 47, 74.

2. See Richard of St. Victor, who was greatly influenced by the Greek Fathers in his writings on the Holy Trinity, *De Trinitate*, 3, 2, ed. Jean Ribaillier; PL 196; 138.

3. Ibid., 147.

4. Athanasius, *Contra Gentes* in A Select Library of Nicene and Post-Nicene Fathers of the Christian Church 41:26.

5. Irenaeus, *Adversus Haereses*, III, 19, 1; 448–49; Athanasius, *De Incarnatione et Contra Arianos*, PG 26; 5; 992.

6. Athanasius, *Ad Serap*. I, 20; PG 26, 5; 992.

7. Ibid., 24; 588B.

8. Ibid., 26; 592B.

9. Ibid., IV, 3; 640–41A.

10. See: George Maloney, S.J., *The Mystic of Fire and Light: St. Symeon the New Theologian* (Denville, N.J.: Dimension Books, 1975).

11. Symeon, *Chapitres théologiques, gnostiques et pratiques*, Sources Chrétiennes 51 (Paris: Cerf, 1965), 3, 45, 9–14; 93.

12. Symeon, *Catecheses*, Sources Chrétiennes 96, ed. Archbishop Basil Krivochene, 24 (Paris: Cerf, 1965), 79–84; 40.

13. *Traités Ethiques*, Sources Chrétiennes 129, ed. and trans. Jean Darrouzes, A.A. (Paris: Cerf, 1965), 3, 546; 428.

14. *Chapitres théologiques, gnostiques et pratiques*, 2, 8; 73.

15. See J. Mahe, "La Sanctification d'après saint Cyrille d'Alexandrie," in *Revue d'Histoire Ecclesiastique* 10 (1909): 480.

16. St. Symeon the New Theologian, "Hymn 44," *Hymns of Divine Love*, trans. G. A. Maloney, S.J. (Denville, N.J.: Dimension Books, 1975), 232.

Epilogue

1. St. Gregory of Nyssa, *De Beatitudine, Oratio VII*, in PG 44; 1280 B–C.

Glossary

Acedia: One of the eight capital sins or vices, the roots of all sins. *Acedia* is the temptation most common to monks and refers to the sadness or boredom that tempts a person to ennui and discouragement in the inner battle that leads to purity of heart.

Agape: Greek for Christian "love," or "charity," as St. Paul describes it in 1 Corinthians 13:1–8. It is also used in the New Testament as a synonym for the Eucharist as the "love-feast."

Alogos: Greek meaning "without the Logos" and first used by Origen in the third century to refer to Satan, who by sin rejected the freedom to live in the Logos in whom the Father creates all things.

Anakephalaiaos: Greek word used by Paul and Eastern writers, especially Irenaeus, meaning "recapitulation." As used by the Greek Fathers it can refer to a "resumé," a taking up of all since the beginning, a return to the source, a restoration, a reorganization and incorporation under one head, Jesus Christ. Christ completes God's eternal plan by overthrowing Satan and the works of sin and gathering all creatures under one head, Christ, to the glory of the Father (see Eph. 1:10).

Apatheia: From Greek *a-pathos,* meaning "dispassion." The goal of most of the Eastern ascetics is to bring into subjection to the indwelling Lord Jesus all human passions, created by God as good, but now directed by sin in us toward submission to the inner sources that make up our "carnal mindedness." *Apatheia* is the state attained through virtue and the control of these inordinate passions so that the individual will act in harmonious obedience to do only God's will in all things.

Apophatism: From the Greek verb *apophanai,* "to speak out or to deny." *Apophatic* is usually translated as "negative" in contrast to *cataphatic* theology, which is one of positive assertions about God in relationship to us human beings, drawn chiefly through Scripture and the use of human rational knowledge. Apophatism denies that such positive knowledge is our only human knowledge about God. More importantly it asserts that there is a positive, experiential knowledge in the mystical order, an infused knowledge given by God to those who are "clean of heart" for they shall "see" or experience God in "luminous darkness."

Arianism: An early Christian heresy begun by the Alexandrian priest Arius, who maintained that Jesus Christ was not the eternal Son of the Father from all eternity. This heresy was condemned in the first two ecumenical councils of Nicaea (325) and Constantinople (381).

Autexousion: From Greek *autos,* "self," and *exousiazo* "to rule, to exert power." This refers to the free will that, in spite of inherited sin, still remains and allows us to be free agents, acting autonomously under the power God has given us by creating us according to his own image and likeness.

Cataphatic: From Greek *kata,* "positive," "according to," and *phanero,* "to assert" or "affirm." It refers to the positive theology that the Eastern Fathers derive from the perfections we find in creatures; from this limited knowledge we are able to know something about the infinite perfections of God.

Divine energies: God in his essence is unknowable by us human beings and is immutable. Yet God as Trinity freely consents to communicate with us in his uncreated divine energies of love. These are not merely God's actions. God-Trinity is one nature yet three distinct persons, communicating each of themselves in the unity of love that allows God, Father, Son, and Spirit, to give us not only created beings, but to give themselves gratuitously as primary grace, free gifts of the divine persons in their active energies immanently at work within each creature.

Eikon: Greek meaning "icon or image." Jesus is the icon or image of the invisible God (Col. 1:15).

Eleutheria: Greek for "freedom." It is the quality that accompanies the "integrated human nature," allowing a person to regain the harmony that God intended for us before sin occurred. It is the divinizing work of the Holy Spirit to restore this harmony as a person is guided by the Spirit to seek only the will of God.

Epectasis: Greek for "stretching out," as St. Paul uses the word "I *stretch out* for what is still to come" (Phil. 3:13). Gregory of Nyssa builds a Christian mysticism of a process of ever-continuing growth, both in this life and in the life to come as we grow "from glory to glory."

Epiklesis: From Greek *epi,* "upon," and *kalein,* "a calling down" of the Holy Spirit in the sacraments, especially the Eucharist, to make the risen Lord Jesus present and effecting what the symbols of the individual sacraments signify.

Eschaton: Greek for "the end" or "the end times" in which God's eternal plan will be fulfilled and the Kingdom of Heaven will be completed in its manifestation of all creatures in Christ to the glory of God.

Gnosis: Greek for "knowledge." It is the foundation for the pre-Christian mystery cults whose esoteric elements were loosely brought into in the early Church.

Gnosticism: From the Greek word, *gnosis,* or "knowledge." It is older than Christianity and represents the fusion of Oriental and Greek ideas into various elaborate systems whose aim was to acquire *gnosis,* or knowledge of the divine. Ancient mythological material was blended with philosophic and religious ideas. In the second century of Christianity it took on a heretical form with the Christian element only a superficial addition to a system already complete. It spread from Edessa and Alexandria and was refuted by many early Christian writers, especially St. Irenaeus of Lyons in his work *Adversus Haereses.*

Godhead: The term used by the early Fathers, especially the Cappadocian Fathers, to refer to the "unoriginated Source" of all being, the ultimate essence of God, which cannot be known through human knowledge.

Harmatia: Greek word that, together with the word *hamartema,* designates the New Testament concept of sin. It is used to describe sin as a single act, as a state or condition, or as a power infecting not only the entire human race, but also the subhuman cosmos.

Hesed: The Hebrew term referring to God's condescending love to make a covenant with his Chosen People. See Genesis 17:2–8.

Hesychasm: This refers to the type of "desert" spirituality that started in the fourth century with the development in the Egyptian and Mesopotamian deserts of various forms of monasticism. Men and women lived a way of life made up of intense ascetical practices of solitude, the guarding of one's thoughts, and purification of the "heart" by fasting, vigils, and incessant prayer which included synchronizing one's breathing with the name of Jesus. The goal was to attain transformation by the uncreated energies of God-Trinity into their divinized true selves as in their humanity they fulfilled God's eternal plan to make all of us in God's image and likeness.

Hesychast: A monk who strove to live according to the desert spirituality of hesychasm.

Hesychia: Greek for "tranquility" or "rest," referring to inner integration between body, soul, and spirit in Christ as the fulfillment of God's plan to create us "according to his own image and likeness" (Gen. 1:26).

Homoiosis: Greek for "likeness." Irenaeus builds a theological anthropology upon the phrases of Genesis 1:26: *kat' eikona,* "according to the image" of God, and *kath' homoiosin,* "according to the likeness" of God. The imageness can never be lost in us, not even through sin, as it is a potential to be evolved into the likeness, which means to discover one's true self in Christ Jesus as an ongoing process into his *likeness.*

Hypostasis: Greek for "person." In Christology it refers to the one, individuated person, the eternal Son of the Father. Through the incarnation he possesses two distinct but inseparable natures, divine and human.

Kata Physin: Greek for "according to human nature." In the thinking of the early Eastern Fathers this phrase referred to everything that God puts into human nature, whether at the beginning stage or the final one. It also refers to, at least in potentiality, all that would come to a human being after baptism and through living a virtuous life. In this manner the Fathers did not write about a supernature imposed upon nature, but rather a "drawing out" of all that God has put into human nature in the beginning.

Kat' eikona: Greek for "according to the image of God."

Kenosis: Greek for "an emptying." In Eastern theology it refers to Paul's description of the central work of Christ as a "self-emptying" of himself in and through his death on the cross (Phil. 2:7), to image in human form the perfect love of the Father for his children, made in Christ's image and likeness.

Logismoi: Greek for "thoughts" or "images." These can be both good and bad. They are sensible phantasms that when dwelt upon may draw a person to that object existing outside of oneself. Given our fallen nature and the distension introduced into us through Original Sin, we are drawn to those things that take us away from doing God's holy will. Guarding against such thoughts on the body, soul, and spiritual levels is a major element of the ascetical life.

Logos: Greek for "word," or the form which expresses a thought as well as the thought itself. The early Greek Fathers built their Christology upon the writings of St. John and St. Paul, who stressed Jesus Christ as the Logos, one with the Godhead from all eternity, who took on our human nature. It is in the Logos in whom all things are created (John 1:2). Therefore every creature possesses a unique *logos* in relationship to the divine Logos, Jesus Christ, who in the end will gather all creatures into himself and bring the universe into its fulfillment as the Father conceived all creatures in and through and for the *divine Logos* made flesh, Jesus Christ.

Macrocosm: From Greek *makros,* "long, great," and *kosmos,* the "cosmos." The Eastern Fathers, especially Irenaeus and Maximus the Confessor, saw the presence of Christ risen and living in his Body, the Church, as recapitulating the entire cosmos into a unity through the power of the Holy Spirit.

Metanoia: From Greek *meta,* "a complete returning to," and *nous,* "mind or heart." It is the Greek word used in the New Testament and the patristic writers of the early Church to indicate an ongoing process of sincere repentance, a complete upheaval of our "carnal" values to put on the mind of Jesus Christ (Eph. 4:17).

Microcosm: From Greek *mikros,* "small," and *kosmos,* "world." The human being is conceived of by the Fathers as a microcosm, a miniature of what the microcosm or the entire world is to become as we are called to be "cocreators" with Christ to bring all creation under Christ, who will bring it to completion back to the Father.

Monophysitism: From Greek *monos,* "one," and *physis,* "nature." It refers to the fifth-century heresy that maintained that there was but a single nature in Christ, i.e., the humanity of Jesus was subsumed into his divinity, or the human and divine natures in Jesus Christ made up only one composite nature. It was condemned in the ecumenical Council of Chalcedon (451).

Monotropoi: From Greek *monos,* "one," and *tropos,* "way," "manner," "style of pursuing a goal." The term was used by the early ascetical writers to describe the monastic life as seeking diligently holiness and perfection as the only goal.

Nepsis: From Greek *nepo,* "to be sober, not to be intoxicated." It refers in Eastern Christian asceticism to the *praxis* of striving to attain a mental sobriety or balance, an inner alertness and attentiveness to seek always to fulfill the divine commandments.

Nestorianism: A fifth-century heresy begun by the Patriarch Nestorius of Constantinople, who maintained that Jesus Christ had two natures, divine and human, but therefore had to be also two persons. Mary was not the birthgiver to God, but rather gave birth to the human person, Jesus, who died on the cross, since God could not suffer and die. This doctrine was condemned in the Council of Ephesus in 431.

Oikonomia: From Greek *oikos,* "house," and *nomos,* "law" or "the right management" of the universe according to the right order God has placed into his creation. In theology it refers to the providential care of God as Trinity working within the universe to evolve all creatures into a unity through the recapitulation of Christ, who will bring all creatures into a harmonious completion in and through his Church, his Body. In Eastern Canon Law this term specifically provides the principle of "oikonomia" or "economy," i.e., God provides within his Church the ability to bring salvation to those in need, within or outside the Church, without sacrificing the ideal principles of Church discipline or teaching.

Orthodoxia: From Greek *orthos,* "right," "correct," and *doxa,* "praise," "glory." It means specifically "right teaching" that brings right glory to God since it corresponds to God's revealed truth.

Orthopraxis: From Greek *orthos,* "right," "correct," and *praxis,* "living." For Eastern Christians right teaching must also be lived out. There can be no intellectual assent given in faith to a revealed truth together with a style of living that does not admit of a faithful response to live according to God's truth.

Para physin: From Greek *para,* "against," and *physis,* "nature." In the thinking of the Eastern writers this term refers to whatever goes "against human nature" or goes parallel to it, but is never in harmony with human nature as God has created it. This is the essence of sin.

Parousia: Greek meaning "presence" or manifestation through a fulfillment or the "arrival" of some person. It denoted the triumphal entry of rulers, kings, emperors, high-ranking magistrates, and religious leaders into a city. St. Paul sees the triumphal entry of Christ in his victorious return to earth at the end of time (1 Thess. 5:2; 2 Thess. 1:7–12; 1 Cor. 15:20–28; 2 Cor. 1:14).

Parrhesia: Greek for "childlike trust" in God. At times the Greek writers applied this term to an excess of trust which led to presumption on God's loving care without a corresponding cooperation on the part of the individual.

Pathos: Greek meaning primarily "passions" created by God that are essentially good. Sin has infected them and created the "passions" that in the spiritual order are diseased and out of harmony with God's initial creation. It usually implies affection, even sympathy for the sufferings of others. But it also can express suffering, a misfortune, animosity, or a grudge toward others.

Penthos: Greek word to express an abiding sorrow for sins. Such "compunction" was considered an essential element in Eastern Christian spirituality, which usually stressed the gift of tears as an indication of a true and lasting state of "conversion."

Philautia: From Greek *phile,* "love," and *autos,* "self." Maximus the Confessor taught that self-love was the root of all sin.

Phthora: Greek "ruin," "waste." The Fathers used this term to describe the "corruptibility" that sin brought into God's creation. It came to mean the deprivation of God's life of grace inherited by the sin of Adam and passed on to all human beings.

Physis: Greek "nature or essence" of a being.

Platonism: The philosophy developed on the writings of Plato, which influenced many of the early Christian writers, especially those of Alexandria, e.g., Origen.

Pleroma: Greek "fullness" or "maturity." In Eastern Christian theology it refers to Christ's influence on the entire created world as redeemed by him and thus arriving gradually at its goal of fullness, which is God in all things and all things in God.

Pneumatomachoi: From Greek *pneuma,* "Spirit," and *machomai,* "to combat," "to fight." The name was given to those who embraced the heresy of the Patriarch Macedonius, who denied the divinity of the Holy Spirit. The heresy was condemned in the second Ecumenical Council of Constantinople (381).

Praxis: Greek "deed," "act," "action." In Eastern Christian ascetical teaching, *praxis* refers to what human beings do in cooperation with God's grace in order to uproot any self-centeredness, called in general the eight "vices," and to put on the mind of Jesus Christ by an inner revolution that develops the virtues he lived by and taught us to imitate.

Prosochi: Greek "attention," "care." In Eastern Christian asceticism it refers to inner vigilance and attention given to the thoughts and movements of the mind and heart in order to bring them into loving submission to God's will.

Ruah: Hebrew "breath" or "wind." A symbol of God's power operating throughout all creation in and through the Spirit.

Soter: Greek "Savior." In Greek Christian theology it refers to Jesus Christ, the Savior.

Soteria: Greek "salvation," "redemption," the bringing of one into safety. In Christianity "soteriology" refers to the branch of theology that seeks to explain how Jesus Christ has brought about the salvation of the human race.

Synergy: From Greek *syn*, "together," "with," and *energeia*, "energy," "a working," "activity." As Jesus worked with his Father (John 5:17), so we are able to work with him in every thought, word, and deed by his indwelling presence in us.

Taboric light: This term refers to the teaching of Gregory Palamas and his successors that purified Christians, due to the uncreated energies of God, are able to be transformed into a sharing of the light that Jesus radiated on Mount Tabor through the process of divinization as they yield to the divine indwelling presence of the Trinity.

Theognosia: From Greek *Theos*, "God," and *gnosis*, "knowledge." The Eastern Fathers in their apophatic theology maintained that, although we can never know God in his essence, yet in the salvific order by God's free choice we can come to a true knowledge and love of God-Trinity through an infusion given by the Holy Spirit to the "poor in spirit."

Theoria physica: Greek *theoria*, "contemplation," and *physica*, referring to all of God's material world. This refers in the writings of Evagrius and Maximus the Confessor to the level of human contemplation of the Logos in whom all things have their ultimate being in God. This is to pass from self-activity to become the subject of divine infusion of a *gnosis* given by the Holy Spirit, who unveils the presence of the Word made flesh, Jesus Christ, who with the Holy Spirit and our human cooperation is bringing all of the created cosmos back to completion in God.

Theoria theologica: Greek *theoria*, "contemplation," and *theologica*, referring to the highest degree of mystical contemplation of the Holy Trinity. Such *gnosis* of the Trinity is the aim of true theology and can be given to us only in the proportion that we are assimilated to the likeness of Christ.

Theosis: The Greek word, coined by Clement of Alexandria in the third century, used to describe the process of divinization whereby we are able to become gods by grace and our cooperation (2 Pet. 1:4).

Theotokos: Greek "Birthgiver to God," applied to Mary as the Mother of God. This doctrine was solemnly defined in the Council of Ephesus (431) to combat Nestorianism, which taught that she gave birth only to the human Jesus.

Transubstantiation: The scholastic theological explanation of how in the consecration of the Eucharist in the Mass Jesus Christ is totally present under the species of bread and wine; the substances of bread and wine disappear, leaving only the total substance of the God-man Jesus Christ.

Bibliography

Ancient Christian Writers. Ed. J. Quasten and J. C. Plumpe. Westminster, Md.

Ante-Nicene Christian Library. Edinburgh.

Ante-Nicene Fathers. Buffalo and New York.

Aumann, J., O.P., ed. *Christian Spirituality East and West*. Chicago, 1968.

Behr-Sigel, M. *La prière a Jésus*. Dieu Vivant 8. Paris, 1948.

Bouyer, L. *The Spirituality of the New Testament and the Fathers*. New York, 1964.

Bria, Bishop I. *Martyria/Mission: The Witness of the Orthodox Churches Today*. Geneva, 1980.

Brianchaninov, Bishop I. *The Prayer of Jesus*. Trans. Lazarus Moore. London, 1952.

Budge, E. A. Wallis, ed. and trans. *The Wit and Wisdom of the Christian Fathers of Egypt*. London, 1934.

Cabasilas, N. *A Commentary on the Divine Liturgy*. Trans. J. M. Hussey and P. A. McNulty. London, 1960.

———. *The Life in Christ*. Trans. C. J. de Catanzaro. Crestwood, N.Y., 1974.

Climacus, John. *The Ladder of Divine Ascent*. Trans. Lazarus Moore. London, 1959.

Daniélou, J., and H. Musurillo, eds. *From Glory to Glory* (texts from Gregory of Nyssa's mystical writings). New York, 1961.

Dictionnaire de Spiritualité. Paris, 1960.

Dionysius, Pseudo-Areopagite. *The Works of Dionysius the Areopagite*. Ed. and trans. John Parker. New York, 1976.

Evagrius of Pontus. *The Praktikos/Chapters on Prayer.* Trans. John Eudes Bamberger, O.C.S.O. Cistercian Studies 4. Spencer, Mass., 1970.

Evdokimov, P. *L'Orthodoxie.* Paris, 1959.

Evergetenos, M. *The Ancient Fathers of the Desert.* Brookline, Mass., 1980.

———. *Holy Mothers of Orthodoxy.* Minneapolis, 1987.

Fedotov, G. P. *A Treasury of Russian Spirituality.* New York, 1948.

Festugière, A. *Contemplation et vie contemplative chez Platon.* Paris, 1958.

Florovsky, G. *The Byzantine Ascetic and Spiritual Fathers.* Belmont, Mass., 1987.

———. *Bible, Church and Tradition.* Belmont, Mass., 1972.

Gregory Palamas. *Les Triades pour la defense des Saints Hésychastes.* Ed. John Meyendorff. 3 vols. Louvain, 1959.

Habra, G. "The Patristic Sources of the Doctrine of Gregory Palamas on the Divine Energies," *Eastern Churches Quarterly* 12 (1957–58).

Hausherr, I. "La méthode d'oraison hésychaste," *Orientalia Christiana* (Rome) 36 (1927): 109–210.

———. "L'origine de la théorie orientale des huit péchés capitaux," *Orientalia Christiana* 30, no. 86 (1933): 164–75.

———. "Les grands courants de la spiritualité orientale," *Orientalia Christiana Periodica* 1 (1935): 114–38.

———. "Penthos, La doctrine de la compunction dans L'Orient chrétien," in Orientalia Christiana Analecta 132. Rome, 1944.

———. "Direction spirituelle en Orient autrefois," in Orientalia Christiana Analecta 144. Rome, 1955.

———. "L'hesychasme, Étude de spiritualité," in *Orientalia Christiana Periodica* 22 (1956): 5–40, 247–85.

———. *Les leçons d'un contemplatif: Le Traité de l'oraison d'Evagre le Pontique.* Paris, 1960.

Heiler, Fr. *Urkirche und Ostkirche.* Munich, 1937.

Igumen Chariton of Valamo, compiler. *The Art of Prayer: An Orthodox Anthology.* Trans. E. Kaloubovsky and E. E. H. Palmer. London, 1966.

Jaeger, W. *Early Christianity and Greek Paideia.* Cambridge, England, 1961.

John of Kronstadt. *My Life in Christ.* Trans. E. E. Goulaeff. London, 1897.

Kadloubovsky, E., and G. Palmer, trans. *Philokalia: Early Fathers from the Philokalia.* London, 1954.

———. *Philokalia: Writings from the Philokalia on Prayer of the Heart.* London, 1951.

———. *Unseen Warfare.* London, 1952.

Krivoshein, Bishop Basil. *The Ascetic and Theological Teaching of Gregory Palamas.* London, 1954.

Lossky, Vladimir. *Mystical Theology of the Eastern Church.* Naperville, Ill., 1957.

———. *Vision of God.* Clayton, Wis., 1963.

Louf, André. *The Message of Monastic Spirituality.* Tournai and New York, 1964.

Maloney, George. *Russian Hesychasm.* The Hague, 1973.

———. *The Mystic of Fire and Light.* Denville, N.J., 1975.

———, ed., and trans. *The Writings of Pseudo-Macarius.* Ed. and Trans. Rahway, N.J., 1992.

McGinn, B., and J. Meyendorff, eds. *Christian Spirituality: Origins to the Twelfth Century.* New York, 1988.

Meyendorff, J. *A Study of Gregory Palamas.* Trans. G. Lawrence. Aylesbury, Bucks., 1964.

———. *St. Gregory and Orthodox Spirituality.* Trans. Adele Fiske. Crestwood, N.Y., 1974.

Meyer, R. *Palladius: The Lausiac History.* Matawan, N.J., 1964.

Migne, J. P., ed. *Patrologia Graeca.* Paris, 1844.

———. *Patrologia Latina.* Paris, 1857–66.

Miguel, P. "La Conscience de la grâce selon Symeon le Nouveau Theologian," *Irénikon* 42 (1969).

Monk of the Eastern Church. *Orthodox Spirituality.* London, 1945.

The Nicene and Post-Nicene Fathers. 2d series. Trans. P. Schaff and H. Wace. Grand Rapids, Mich.

Palmer, G., P. Sherrard, and K. Ware, eds. *The Philokalia.* 3 vols. London, 1979ff.

Payne, R. *The Holy Fire: The Story of the Fathers of the Eastern Church.* Crestwood, N.Y., 1980.

Raya, J., and J. de Vinck, eds. *The Byzantine Daily Worship.* Allendale, N.J., 1969.

Schmemann, A. *Sacraments and Orthodoxy.* New York, 1965.

Spidlik, T. *The Spirituality of the Christian East.* Kalamazoo, Mich., 1986.

Symeon the New Theologian. *The Discourses.* Trans. C. J. Catanzaro. New York, 1980.

――――. *Hymns of Divine Love.* Trans. G. A. Maloney. Denville, N.J., 1974.

Vanneste, J. *Le Mystère de Dieu: Essai sur la structure rationelle de la doctrine mystique du Pseudo-Denys l'Aréopagite.* Paris, 1959.

Voobus, A. *A History of Asceticism in the Syrian Orient.* 2 vols. in Corpus Scriptorum Christianorum Orientalium. Paris.

Waddell, H. *The Desert Fathers.* London, 1936.

The Way of a Pilgrim. Trans. R. M. French. London, 1954.

Ward, B. *The Desert Christian: Sayings of the Desert Fathers.* New York, 1975.

OF RELATED INTEREST

Edited by Bernard McGinn, John Meyendorff, and Jean Leclercq
CHRISTIAN SPIRITUALITY
Volume I: Origins to the Twelfth Century
"In less than five hundred breathless pages, an international array
of scholars sketches significant aspects of Christian spirituality
from the birth of Jesus to the twelfth century in both the
Eastern and Western Churches." — *Library Journal*
0-8245-0847-5; $24.95

Edited by Jill Raitt in collaboration with
Bernard McGinn and John Meyendorff
CHRISTIAN SPIRITUALITY
Volume II: High Middle Ages and Reformation
"An excellent study of medieval and reformational spirituality from
1150 to 1600.... The scholarship is of the highest caliber.
Highly recommended." — *Choice*
0-8245-0967-6; $24.95

Edited by Louis Dupre and Don E. Saliers
in collaboration with John Meyendorff
CHRISTIAN SPIRITUALITY
Volume III: Post-Reformation and Modern
"One could scarcely expect more laudable treatments of the persons and
movements selected than one will find here." — *Review and Expositor*
0-8245-0847-5; $24.95

*At your bookstore or, to order directly from the publisher, please send check or money
order (including $3.00 shipping for the first book and $1.00 for each additional book) to:*

THE CROSSROAD PUBLISHING COMPANY
370 LEXINGTON AVENUE, NEW YORK, NY 10017

We hope you enjoyed Gold, Frankincense, and Myrrh. *Thank you for reading it.*

crossroad